Iraqi soldiers in Iran, 1980.

To The American People: How To Use This Book

Hostage to Khomeini was designed in summer 1980 as an indictment of President Carter's role in contributing to the downfall of the Shah and Khomeini's seizure of power. It was—and is—a story that the American people desperately need to know.

Now, in 1981, this book must be used to great effect with the incoming government of Ronald Reagan. It is the political responsibility of the American people, once informed, to act in concert to prevent the next U.S. administration from repeating the mistakes of the previous one. An opportunity exists for the entire Khomeini regime to be swept away during 1981 and replaced with a government of sanity.

But that will depend on the will of the American citizenry. Buy two copies of this book, and send one to your congressman. Ask your local bookseller to keep it in stock. Ask your local newspaper to review it.

Let the officials in Washington know that the American people will not tolerate our government treating the Khomeini regime as anything but the outlaw dictatorship that it is.

—*January 1, 1981*

To the American People: How To Use This Book

Hostage to Khomeini

Hostage to Khomeini

by Robert Dreyfuss

with Thierry LeMarc

New Benjamin Franklin House
Publishing Company
New York

Hostage to Khomeini
Published by the New Benjamin Franklin House
  Publishing Company, Inc.
Copyright © 1980 by Robert Dreyfuss

FIRST EDITION

For information contact the publisher:
The New Benjamin Franklin House
  Publishing Company
304 West 58th Street
New York 10019

Library of Congress Cataloging in Publication
  Hostage to Khomeini
    1. Iran—Politics and government—1941-1979.
2. Iran—Politics and government—1979-
3. Khumaynī, Rūh Allāh.   I. Title.
DS318.D73   955,.053   80-24288
ISBN 0-933488-11-4

Designed by Gail Kay
Cover design by Alan Yue

Photo front cover: Sygma/Alain Dejean
Photo back cover: James Morehead/Blackstone

PRINTED IN THE UNITED STATES OF AMERICA

Contents

Illustrations follow page 127.

Author's Preface

The writing of this book was commissioned by Lyndon H. LaRouche, founding editor of the *Executive Intelligence Review*, as an indispensable contribution to the political education of the American people.

Perhaps more than any other individual, LaRouche has succeeded in driving home the simple truth that Ayatollah Khomeini represents a fundamental, moral evil. At a time when the American ambassador to the United Nations was calling Khomeini "a saint" and President Carter himself was describing Khomeini's gang of cutthroats as "our friends," LaRouche identified Khomeini as an immoral and vindictive old man whose perverted brand of Islam bears no relation at all to real religion.

But the origins of Khomeini seemed to be a mystery. How is it possible an obsessive, fanatical mullah could topple the mighty Shah of Iran? Newspapers and other media shed no light on Khomeini's origins; to many, it seemed that he came from nowhere. This unenlightened state prevailed even among the top-most officials of the fallen regime, who had been thrown into exile without a clue as to how the Iranian revolution toppled the Peacock Throne. It is said that even the late Shah of Iran himself really never knew what hit him—until he read the *Executive Intelligence Review*.

But there is really no mystery about the method by which the *Review* discovered the "secret" behind Khomeini.

The key to unlocking the otherwise apparent puzzle of the Khomeini revolution is LaRouche's identification of the worldwide battle between the representatives of the so-called New Dark Ages faction and those forces who are seeking to unleash a new era of unlimited growth and industrialization throughout the world. Certainly, the existence of the Dark Ages faction is no secret, explained LaRouche: for several centuries the British-centered oligarchy has been spreading its gospel of opposition to progress, of deliberate fostering of backwardness and religious cultism. The British economists and social scientists—who like Parson Malthus gave the name "the dismal science" to economics—have argued in a chain stretching back into the seventeenth century that science and technology are evil. For them, the Chinese model of large, beast-like peasant populations laboring under semi-feudal fiefdoms is the only "stable" form of social organization.

It is the British, and their followers, who today hold up China as the ideal for the developing countries of the

Third World. And it is the British who sponsored Ayatollah Khomeini's assault on the twentieth century in Iran.

Once that simple idea is understood, then the masses of detail on exactly how the Iranian revolution took place can easily be sorted out. Khomeini, in fact, did not make a revolution. He was put in power from the outside, as a convenient front man for a Dark Ages transformation of Iran. Like the mythical Wizard of Oz, Khomeini is a puffed up, turbaned magician who has enchanted far too many of Iran's unfortunate peasant population and its youth—but he was installed, like a light bulb, by a carefully orchestrated British Military Intelligence operation.

This book tells that story. It also chronicles the treasonous role of the Carter administration in collaborating with the British in putting Khomeini into power. The book is intended to serve as an indictment of a highly placed fifth column inside the United States who provided aid and comfort to the monstrous ayatollahs and their secret society, the Muslim Brotherhood—even after the taking of the American embassy in Teheran!

Not until Jimmy Carter, Zbigniew Brzezinski, Henry Kissinger, Ramsey Clark, and Cyrus Vance are in prison will this volume have served its purpose.

And not until the entire organization of the Muslim Brotherhood worldwide, from its underground terrorist cells in the Middle East, to its exile headquarters in London, Geneva, and Malta, to its backers at prestigious universities like Georgetown University in Washington, D.C., is hunted down and destroyed will the countries of the Muslim world be safe from the Khomeini disease.

In closing, I wish to acknowledge the exciting and

rewarding collaboration of my friends and colleagues at the *Executive Intelligence Review*. As the Middle East intelligence director of the *EIR*, it has been my privilege to enjoy the assistance of experienced analysts Mark Burdman, Judith Wyer, and Nancy Coker. In addition, I wish to acknowledge the invaluable aid of my co-author, Thierry Le Marc, *EIR*'s European bureau Middle East chief.

And, in particular, I wish to thank Criton Zoakos and Christopher R. White, *EIR*'s political intelligence directors, for their inspiration and support.

Robert Carmen Dreyfuss
November 7, 1980
New York City

Hostage to Khomeini

1

The
Revolution
By 'Our Friends'

In Teheran, uncontrolled mobs surge through the streets brandishing their newly acquired automatic weapons, sacking public buildings and tearing down the remains of the regime of the deposed Shah. The bloody reign of terror has already begun. Quickly and silently, top military and intelligence officers who have refused to cooperate with the new government are executed by unofficial assassination squads. In the cities, as in the towns and villages, many hundreds more are murdered by frenzied crowds. It is February 12, 1979, just hours after the Ayatollah Khomeini has proclaimed the establishment of the Islamic Republic of Iran.

In Washington, President Carter convenes a hurried news conference to tell the world, "I believe the people of Iran and the government will continue to be our friends."

1

Many people are shocked by Carter's willingness to befriend the bloody new regime. But the President's statement goes little noticed amid the international crisis swirling around the revolution in Iran. A few days later, when an organized band of hoodlums briefly seizes and ransacks the American embassy in Teheran, Carter's remark would seem an ironic footnote in the gathering storm of hatred and fanaticism whipped up by the ayatollah and his Revolutionary Council. In reality, the President's official welcome to the Khomeini dictatorship signaled a far deeper truth. Carter had great reason to believe that the regime of the mullahs in Iran would indeed be "our friend": He and his administration had put Khomeini in power.

Not simply by inaction. The Carter administration—with sober deliberation and with malice aforethought—had given aid to the movement that organized the overthrow of the Shah of Iran. The Carter administration was involved every step of the way—from the propaganda preparations to the supply of arms and ammunition, from the behind-the-scenes deals with traitors in the Shah's military to the final ultimatum to the beaten leader in January 1979 to leave Iran. Perhaps no other chapter in American history is so replete with treachery to the ideals upon which the nation was founded.

The real story of Iran's revolution is a tale that makes spy stories like Paul Erdman's *The Crash of '79* seem tame by comparison. It is necessary to look behind the closed doors of the world's most powerful and prestigious banks, oil companies, and industrial corporations and into the paneled board rooms of elite clubs such as the New York Council on Foreign Relations and the Royal Institute of International Affairs in London. Iran is the battleground for a behind-the-scenes war that is still raging among international circles of high finance and their friends in the various intelligence services of the NATO countries, Israel, and the Middle East.

Within the United States government, a relatively small group of managers is responsible for the downfall of the Shah. Heading the list are Zbigniew Brzezinski of the National Security Council, former Secretary of State Cyrus Vance, and the NSC's Iran Task Force special coordinator, George Ball. Also involved are David Newsom and Henry Precht of the State Department, along with U.S. Ambassador William H. Sullivan in Teheran; Harold Brown and Charles Duncan at the Pentagon; General Alexander Haig and General Robert Huyser of NATO's command; and the Central Intelligence Agency's Admiral Stansfield Turner and Robert Bowie.

Working under this administrative elite is a stable of Middle East and Iran specialists with long experience in the field. We can name Richard Cottam of the University of Pittsburgh; Marvin Zonis of the University of Chicago; James Bill of the University of Texas at Austin; Richard Falk and Bernard Lewis of Princeton; and Thomas Ricks of Georgetown University. Together with a select group of British intelligence agents and representatives of the secret society called the Muslim Brotherhood, this group acted, from 1977 to 1979, as the liaison between the on-the-ground organizers of the Khomeini revolution and the Carter White House and the National Security Council. Coordinator for the operation was former U.S. attorney general Ramsey Clark.

As President Carter in January 1978 was embracing the Shah and praising Iran as an "island of stability" in the turbulent Middle East, his aides were already working to hurl this ally of the United States into the tumult of revolution.

As early as 1977, numbers of officials in the Carter administration were aware that the United States was quietly giving support to the forces opposed to the Shah that were then gathering around the Ayatollah Khomeini. But only a few knew the strategy behind the ongoing U.S. intelligence contacts with Khomeini's advisers. The information was highly secret and was provided only on a "need to know" basis; dozens of low-level functionaries at the State Department, the Pentagon, and the CIA operated partially or almost totally in the dark. To them, it seemed clear only that the developing alliance between the White House and the Muslim Brotherhood must be part of a geopolitical strategy aimed at the Soviet Union.

For the naive, superficial explanations were provided. During 1978, for example, rumors began to circulate in the intelligence community in Washington that the CIA had detected the fact that the Shah had cancer and that, despite treatments, he would soon die. In this version, the death of the Shah would leave a leadership gap in Iran that could not easily be filled by the normal succession process. In the expected chaos, the CIA was said to believe, the Soviet Union could take advantage of Iran's crisis to intervene. It was argued that the United States must begin contacts with the opposition to the Shah—which was primarily religious-based—to prepare a replacement government. This story may have satisfied junior officers in the government bureaucracy who noticed, little by little, the growing pattern of overt and covert U.S. links with the radical anti-Shah forces.

The American people were told nothing.

The driving force in the Carter administration behind the "Islamic card" against the Soviet Union was National Security chief Zbigniew Brzezinski. Since 1977, Brzezinski had declared in public his view that "Islamic fundamentalism" is a "bulwark against communism." In an interview with the *New York Times* after the Iranian revolution, Brzezinski proclaimed that Washington should "welcome" the resurgent force of Islam in the Middle East because, as an ideology, it was in conflict with those forces in the area that were potential supporters of the Soviet Union. This view was reaffirmed by Carter press secretary Jody Powell on November 7, 1979, three days after the taking of fifty-three American hostages in Iran.

Although Brzezinski is reliably reported to be almost totally unfamiliar with political conditions in the Middle East, he has had a steady preoccupation with the use of religions and religious cults as a tool of political warfare. Trained by the Jesuits at McGill University—he has stated that he considers himself so close to the Jesuits in his method of thinking that he is almost a honorary member of the Society—and obsessed, because of his background as a member of the reactionary aristocracy of feudal Poland, with the liberation of Eastern Europe, he has explored the potential for an uprising there led by Jesuit networks. From this vantage point, it was not hard for Brzezinski to leap to the conclusion that a chain of Muslim Brotherhood governments in the Middle East might serve the same purpose there.

Combined with the cultivation of the Jesuit networks and various Eastern European exiles, and the development of the grandiose "China card" in Asia, collaboration with the Muslim Brotherhood would potentially complete the encirclement of the U.S.S.R. with hostile, ideologically committed armies.

Although the strategy, in Brzezinski's view, had great tactical advantages, it was not necessarily aimed at bearing fruit until the passage of perhaps ten or twenty years. During this time, the NSC chief calculated, the gradual weakening of the Soviet Union as the result of another arms race and persistent economic warfare would lead to the eventual disintegration of the Soviet Union itself! According to an official U.S. government strategic survey published in 1979, the loyalties of Soviet Muslim citizens to organizations based outside the U.S.S.R. along its southern flank might be an important aid in pulling apart the Soviet Union in the wake of a general thermonuclear war.

Possessed by such doomsday fantasies, Brzezinski's National Security Council commissioned studies for its Special Coordinating Committee on the possible effects of an Islamic resurgence upon the Muslim populations within the borders of the Soviet Union. Up to 50 million Soviets, or one-quarter of the population of the U.S.S.R., are Muslim, and studies produced in London claimed that the country's Muslim component is the fastest growing part of its disparate demographic makeup. According to the *London Times*, which reported these surveys, many Soviet Muslims belong to a secret underground network of Sufi mystical organizations and Muslim brotherhoods. The claim has been refuted by more sober analysts.

But in December 1979, as the revolutionary upsurge against the Shah accelerated, the NSC's Special Coordinating Committee secretly decided to vastly expand the broadcasts of CIA radio stations in languages spoken in Soviet Muslim areas. The following month, Carter administration officials informed the Senate Foreign Relations Committee that Brzezinski had demanded a "worldwide study" of Islamic fundamentalism because of its "growing political impact . . . in many parts of the world." According to the *Washington Post*, Brzezinski "formally directed the intelligence community to produce an in-depth study of this phenomenon."

Gradually, Brzezinski's "Islamic card" came to dominate the policy of the United States toward the entire Middle East. At the height of the revolution against the Shah, Brzezinski issued his famous proclamation that the region was an "Arc of Crisis" stretching from North and East Africa through the Middle East, Turkey, Iran, and Pakistan. In this part of the world, Brzezinski charged, the Soviet Union was making a power play for the oil resources of the Gulf on which the industry of the West was dependent. Although no one seriously believed that Moscow was supporting Khomeini against the Shah— indeed, most analysts thought that Moscow wanted the Shah to remain in power—Brzezinski used the image of the Soviet bear pressing down toward the Indian Ocean to propose the creation of a "Middle East Treaty Organization," or METO.

The idea was not new. In July 1978, Edgar Bronfman, the Zionist head of Seagram's, in an unusual *New York Times* opinion column, had demanded its consideration again. Bronfman disclosed that he had discussed the idea with New York's Senator Jacob Javits and Vice-President Walter Mondale, who then suggested to Brzezinski that it be pursued by the administration. After the proposal was approved as a working paper by the White House, it led to the convening of the Camp David summit in September 1978.

Egypt and Israel were expected to act as the initiating countries for the expansion of NATO into the Middle East. Iran was to be the next link.

In its early stages, METO was to be a loosely organized and informal protocol—resting chiefly on collaboration between national branches of the pan-Islamic Muslim Brotherhood and Israeli intelligence. Brzezinski regarded the Brotherhood as the common factor that could link the disparate regimes in the "Arc of Crisis."

The culmination of Brzezinski's Islamic strategy was the covert American and open Chinese support for the Afghanistan guerrillas operating out of Pakistan and Iran. With the victory of the Islamic revolution in Iran, the fundamentalist guerrillas against the pro-Soviet Afghanistan government were deluged with American aid, as Brzezinski's NSC was fed glowing reports of alleged military victories by the Muslim Brotherhood rebels. Now obsessed with visions of a stunning Islamic victory against the Afghan regime of Prime Minister Amin, Brzezinski and his Peking allies pressed on with the *jihad* (holy war) in Afghanistan—despite the signs in late 1979 that the Soviet Union was preparing military intervention.

When it finally came, the Soviet invasion of Afghanistan was a shock to Brzezinski and the NSC, but it may also have been secretly welcomed; now Washington had the opportunity to mobilize Iran and the rest of the Muslim world against the U.S.S.R., which was portrayed in official Washington statements as Islam's chief enemy.

No matter that Brzezinski's Muslim "allies" had seized the American embassy, held its diplomats hostage, and burned down American embassies in Pakistan and Libya.

The secret of the Ayatollah Khomeini's revolution does not end with the strategic scenarios of "Rasputin" Brzezinski. As the Islamic fundamentalist upsurge was numbering the days of his regime, the Shah of Iran was denouncing not the U.S. National Security Council, but British Petroleum and the British Broadcasting Corporation as the foreign fomenters of rebellion. Brzezinski was playing an "Islamic card" that had been placed in his hand by the British.

By British we do not mean the government of the United Kingdom—but the ruling families of the British oligarchy, which since 1660 have ruled Britain, unchallenged, as the command center for the European feudal nobility and its associated financial interests. Policy for the oligarchy is formulated and conduited through such institutions as the Royal Institute of International Affairs, the International Institute of Strategic Studies, and in the United States through such prestigious organizations as the New York Council on Foreign Relations and the Aspen Institute, among others.

Since the era of Charlemagne, when humanity began pulling itself out of the mud of the dark ages that followed the collapse of the Roman Empire, the gravest danger to Europe's noble families has been posed by the nation-state with a leadership committed to the development of its citizenry and its economy. As the American Revolution proved, an educated population will not tolerate the rule of the oligarchy and its regimen of enforced backwardness.

The scions of Britain's oligarchical families think not in terms of months and years, but in terms of decades and even centuries. The establishment of the Islamic Republic of Iran, for them, was to be the harbinger of a coming era in which religious fundamentalism and an antiscientific world view will prevail. Passed on from generation to generation, the mind of the British aristocrat—like that of his Italian, Dutch, Hapsburg, and other counterparts—is shaped by the belief in the supreme preferability of the days of the lordly manors and feudal estates, when only the nobility, the clergy, and the serfs existed in hierarchically defined relationships.

It is efficient here to quote Lord Bertrand Russell, whose Bertrand Russell Peace Foundation did so much to bring Khomeini to power, to give the reader a glimpse of the kind of mind we are talking about. Writing in his 1951 *Impact of Science on Society*, Russell speaks of the future:

"At present the population of the world is increasing at about 58,000 per diem. War, so far, has had no very great effect on this increase, which continued throughout each of the world wars. . . . War . . . has hitherto been disappointing in this respect . . . but perhaps bacteriological war may prove more effective. If a Black Death could spread throughout the world once in every generation, survivors could procreate freely without making the world too full. . . . The state of affairs might be somewhat unpleasant, but what of it? Really high-minded people are indifferent to happiness, especially other people's. . . . The present urban and industrial centers will have become derelict, and their inhabitants, if still alive, will have reverted to the peasant hardships of their medieval ancestors."

For the oligarchy, the Khomeini regime—which has leveled the Iranian economy and turned its potential citizens into rampaging mobs—is the "shape of things to come." The destruction of Iran's cities, the forced reversion of Iran to an agricultural rather than an industrially developing nation, the cancellation of Iran's nuclear energy program by Khomeini have been praised by representatives of Britain's ruling class not only as a model for the underdeveloped sector but for the Western industrial nations as well.

There is no tactic, no geopolitical strategy of the British oligarchy, that, in the final analysis, is not subordinated to that long-term goal.

But this project might remain simply the anachronistic dream of a class of men who had long outlived their usefulness were it not for the fact that the British dark ages policy has secured hegemony over most of the policy-making apparatus of the United States. That includes the United States government. It is the policy that stands behind such slogans as "postindustrial society," "zero growth," "environmentalism," and the "do your own thing" amorality of the mind-destroying drug-rock counterculture.

In 1975, the British dark ages policy was officially incorporated into the future administration of Jimmy Carter in the form of the Council on Foreign Relations' *1980s Project*, a thirty-volume prospectus for the next decade. Participants of the *1980s Project*—Cyrus Vance, Anthony Solomon, Harold Brown, Zbigniew Brzezinski, Leslie Gelb, among others—moved to Washington with the Carter administration in 1977.

The general theme of the *1980s Project* is "controlled disintegration" of the world economy; the report does not attempt to hide the famine, social chaos, and death this policy will bring upon most of the world's population.

Not made public until 1979, the *1980s Project* papers explained that the world financial and economic system needed a complete overhaul, according to which control of key sectors such as energy, credit allocation, and food would be placed under the direction of a single, global administration. Overseeing the apparatus suggested by the Council would be a team of corporate managers drawn from the ranks of the oil multinationals and Anglo-American banks.

The objective of this reorganization would be the replacement of the nation-state and the global supervision of the United Nations and the International Monetary Fund. This would be accomplished first by dividing the world into separate, regional currency zones, or blocs. There would be a zone in which the bankrupt British pound sterling would be dominant, another for the French franc, another for the U.S. dollar, Japanese yen, and Arab dinar, and so forth. Mediating between each of these zones would be the International Monetary Fund, which would retain nearly complete control over flows of currency and world trade. The U.S. dollar would no longer serve as the world's central reserve currency.

The flow of advanced sector technology into the underdeveloped nations would be halted.

The underdeveloped world would be permitted only what the World Bank calls "appropriate technologies," that is, back-breaking labor-intensive "technology." The International Monetary Fund alone would determine whether a developing nation would be considered "credit-worthy" enough for foreign financial assistance and long-term loans.

Official IMF documents and World Bank studies project that the effect of this program will be a sudden and sharp reduction in population in the Third World. The U.S. State Department-sponsored *Global 2000 Report*, for example, projects—and approves—that this policy will reduce by 3 billion the world's population in the year 2000.

Iran is the test-tube experiment to prove that Third World populations can be made to impose this policy upon themselves.

It would also be a mistake to take at face value Zbigniew Brzezinski's declarations that the primary target of the Carter administration's alliance with Islamic fundamentalism is the Soviet Union. The primary target is the economies of America's allies in Western Europe. And the primary weapon is oil.

In 1978, the governments of France and West Germany led the European Community—with the single exception of Great Britain—in the formation of the European Monetary System, conceived, as one West German official put it, as a "seed crystal for the replacement of the International Monetary Fund." The EMS and its "Phase Two" European Monetary Fund embodied a program that challenged the "controlled disintegration" scenario of the Carter administration at every point, calling for the strengthening of the U.S. dollar, a return to the gold standard, expansion of nuclear energy production around the globe, and the revitalization of the industries of the advanced sector through an ambitious high-technology export program to industrialize the underdeveloped sector.

The success of the new monetary system hinges on forging an alliance for development with the OPEC nations. As early as 1977, France and West Germany had begun exploring the possibility of concretizing a deal with the oil-producing countries in which Western Europe would supply high-technology exports to the OPEC countries in exchange for long-term oil supply contracts at a stable price. In turn, the OPEC countries would deposit their enormous financial surpluses in Western European banks and, eventually, into the EMS's own institutions, which would then relend them to other countries in the Third world. With those credits, the underdeveloped countries could begin to gain access to European high-technology exports.

When London discovered that it could not dissuade President Giscard d'Estaing and West German Chancellor Helmut Schmidt from the EMS project in 1978—using ordinary deterrents—the green light was given to the Muslim Brotherhood to speed the destabilization of Iran.

The chief countries of Western Europe, along with Japan, are almost totally dependent upon their oil supply from the Persian Gulf, and during 1978 that supply came from five states: Iran, Saudi Arabia, Iraq, Kuwait, and the United Arab Emirates. By bringing down the Shah and spreading chaos throughout the Middle East, the Anglo-Americans calculated they could knock out Europe with the threat or actuality of an oil cut-off.

In October 1979, less than a month before the taking of American hostages in Teheran, *Business Week* made the threat public:

"It may be that an Arab banking system funneling petrodollars through the European Monetary System will replace the current domination of the world's financial system by U.S. banks and the IMF. This depends, of course, on OPEC's willingness to play the power-broker part. If it refuses, there is another scenario that many still think unthinkable: open warfare, in which either the industrial West as a group, or the U.S. acting alone, gives up trying to work with OPEC and instead invades the oil fields."

An invasion, of course, would not be calculated to seize the oil supply for the United States—but to deny it to Western Europe and Japan. The body blow to the Western European economies would knock out the European Monetary System. Since the taking of American hostages, this threat has been held over the head of the EMS like the sword of Damocles.

Brzezinski's "Islamic card" has functioned as the most brutal end of the policy the Carter administration brought into the White House. One of the first actions Carter took when he assumed office in January 1977 was to dispatch Vice-President Walter Mondale to France and West Germany to tell the leaders of those two nations that the United States would henceforth oppose the sale of nuclear energy technology to the Third World. West Germany's nuclear deal with Brazil and France's promise to sell nuclear technology to Pakistan came under heavy attack. In Iran, whose Shah had pledged to bring Iran into the ranks of the world's top ten industrial nations by the year 2000, a comprehensive nuclear development program, primarily backed by France and West Germany, was already underway.

Today the Shah's nuclear cooling towers are used as silos for grain, and "Iranization" has become a blackmail threat against every Third World government seeking to industrialize.

It is no idle threat. The capability for the Khomeini revolution has been patiently set in place by the British over a period of years—ready to come to the fore once the decision to destroy Iran had been made.

Were we to select a date for the beginning of the Khomeini revolution, it would be November 1976. It was in that month that Amnesty International, the worldwide "human rights" organization issued its report charging brutality and torture of political prisoners by the Shah of Iran.

True, the groundwork for the Iranian revolution had been laid several years earlier by the Colorado-based Aspen Institute. And the project to destabilize the Shah's regime was rooted in a century or more of Iranian history, during which time British intelligence specialists had cultivated the Iranian clergy, secret societies, and religious brotherhoods as assets of the British Empire. But the Amnesty International report was the gunshot that started the war; one of Washington's staunchest allies had been declared to be expendable.

During the late sixties and early seventies, under the direction of first the State Department's Eugene Rostow and then Henry Kissinger of the National Security Council, the Shah had set his country on a course toward militarization, equipped to be the protector of British and Anglo-American interests in the Persian Gulf region. London and Washington also intended to prevent Iran from engaging in policies that in any way might threaten the exclusive hegemony of the Anglo-American oil and financial interests. During the 1950s and 1960s, for instance, he had involved himself in petroleum deals outside the framework of the Anglo-American oil cartel headed by British Petroleum. The Shah had struck an alliance with Italy's Enrico Mattei in the late 1950s, the head of the state-owned ENI corporation, enraging London; he had also made approaches to the Soviet Union for economic agreements.

The Rostow-Kissinger policy had the full cooperation of Israel's foreign intelligence service, the Mossad.

The team that drew up the plans for expanding Anglo-American military presence in Iran included Robert W. Komer, presently the Undersecretary of Defense for Policy under President Carter. At that time, Komer, who had been a specialist in the Indian Ocean since the Kennedy administration, was working on a joint task force with the British government to plan Anglo-American strategy in the wake of British military withdrawal from the Arabian Gulf countries between 1968 and 1971. Today, Komer is the man behind the so-called Rapid Deployment Force, the special 110,000-man strike force whose primary mission is to seize areas in the Gulf.

Playing on a psychological profile of the Shah drawn by the CIA and British intelligence, the Kissinger State Department convinced the Shah that he had great need for immense amounts of military hardware. With the hardware came unlimited numbers of U.S. and British intelligence personnel; scores of Iranian officers arrived in the United States, Britain, and even Israel for training.

After 1973, however, with the sudden rise of oil prices, the Shah began to see an opportunity for independent action. The 1973-1974 oil hoax was the work of Henry Kissinger. During the December 1973 OPEC meeting in Teheran, the secretary of state had told the Shah to demand an astronomical price increase. Kissinger was acting on behalf of the Seven Sisters oil cartel and the City of London banks, who desired high prices, but the Shah saw the price increases as a way to begin to pull his country out of backwardness. To the intense irritation of his sponsors, the holder of the Peacock Throne began talking about making Iran the "world's sixth industrial power" in one generation.

The Shah's first open challenge to Kissinger came in 1975. With the mediation of President Houari Boumedienne of Algeria and King Faisal of Saudi Arabia, Iran signed a pact with neighboring Iraq that ended a war of attrition waged by the Kurdish minority of Iraq. The Kurdish rebellion was a prized project of the CIA— whose former director, Richard Helms, was ambassador to Iran—the British Secret Intelligence Service, and the Mossad. According to Arab sources, Ayatollah Khomeini in 1975 was in exile in Iraq and supported the Kurdish rebellion against his Iraqi hosts. When the Shah closed the door on the Kurds, Kissinger hit the ceiling. Millions of dollars in logistical support and arms went down the drain in Kurdistan, as the Iraqi armed forces lost no time in mopping up the remnants of the rebellion. Killing or arresting the Kurdish feudal leaders who led the revolt, the Iraqi government moved into Kurdistan with economic development projects, and today Kurdistan is one of the fastest growing parts of the developing sector. For the British and the CIA, the Iran-Iraq pact was an ungrateful slap in the face.

In 1977, things took a more serious turn. Gradually, the Shah began to distance Iran from its close identification with Israel and to loosen the bonds between Iran and the Israeli secret services. Simultaneously, he steered his country into a closer partnership with the Arabs, especially Iraq and Saudi Arabia, cemented at OPEC meetings in 1977 and 1978. Iran executed an astonishing volte-face in OPEC, dropping its longstanding demand for higher prices. In a press conference in 1977, the Shah startled the world by stating his intention to work for oil price stability. Together, Saudi Arabia and Iran produced nearly half of OPEC's entire output; were they to agree on a policy perspective it would be rammed through OPEC councils despite objections from the radicals like Libya.

At the same time, the Shah—who for years had said that he favored dropping the U.S. dollar in favor of a "basket of currencies"—announced that henceforth Iran would support the continued use of the dollar as a means of payment and pricing for oil exports in OPEC.

For several years Kissinger and the British had been trying to convince OPEC to switch to the International Monetary Fund's Special Drawing Rights or a similar unit of account. Saudi Arabia had resisted that policy; until now, Iran had supported it. Then, Saudi King Khalid paid an unprecedented visit to Teheran, where he arranged Saudi financial support for the Iranians.

The Shah's shift in policy reflected not only his desire to strike a more independent course for his country. The Shah was committing Iran to a strategy of closer collaboration with France and West Germany, on the eve of the founding of the European Monetary System. If the Iran-Iraq-Saudi axis had established a permanent working relationship with the EMS, it would have assembled an unstoppable combination against London. Signs had long been emerging of Iranian willingness to become involved with West Germany and France economically. Iran's huge, multibillion dollar nuclear development program was primarily organized in cooperation with Paris and Bonn. Washington had refused to sell advanced nuclear technology to Iran at all!

One deal in particular angered the Anglo-Americans: the three-cornered deal by which Iran agreed to supply the Soviet Union with huge quantities of natural gas, while the U.S.S.R. supplied an equal quantity from its own gas fields to West Germany. The Shah visited Moscow to discuss an expansion of Iran-Soviet economic cooperation.

As far as Washington and London were concerned, he was already a dead man.

The Iranian revolution was more a project in psychological warfare than a matter of street-fighting, and it was directed not from the mosques of rebelling mullahs but from British Secret Intelligence Service headquarters at the Tavistock Institute for Human Relations at Sussex University.

Armed with computers and reams of files on previous experiments in mass brainwashing in Iran, teams of Tavistock social psychologists began to plan the specifics of the "revolution." How would Iranians respond to a call from a decrepit old mullah to revolt? How would the peasants respond? Skilled workers? The middle class? Intellectuals? What techniques would best involve the students in the rebellion? What were the vulnerabilities of the police and armed forces? All this had to be analyzed and taken into account.

The team that was put on the case were men who were experienced in advanced psywar techniques for the

British Secret Intelligence Service going back to the days of World War II and the Strategic Bombing Survey. Experts such as Marvin Zonis, a professor at the University of Chicago who had written *The Political Elite of Iran*, were drawn in to present profiles of how Iranian classes and specific people would react.

The Shah was almost a perfect victim. According to almost every Iranian who has had access to the inner circles of the Shah's court, the Iranian elite was unrivaled in corruption and venality. The Shah's own family was notorious for not caring for the state as much as for the opportunities it offered for shady business deals, smuggling, real estate speculation, and the glittering gold of the international "jet set." Most of the royal family and their friends in Iran were more at home in Acapulco, the French Riviera, or Switzerland than in offices in Teheran. Instead of collecting around him a team of political, economic, and military advisers, the Shah was more wont to surround himself with a clique of fawning sycophants whose only wish was to flatter or praise him in the hopes of securing some greater position of wealth or power.

The Shah refused time and time again to purge his courtiers. His own sense of inadequacy and inferiority, which stemmed from the bitter memories of the British dumping of his father, Reza Shah, in 1941, and his own puppet-like crowning, had led him to overcompensate with an imperial ego and haughty manner. He was unable either to tolerate the rise of potential political rivals or to crack the whip on his immediate circle. It was not unusual for the Shah to clash with advisers and military commanders who would be urging him to take steps necessary to strengthen Iran, and then for these advisers to be removed summarily from their posts. More often than not, the way to get ahead in Iran was to flatter the Shah.

For this reason, many of Iran's most dynamic leaders, particularly those who could see the catastrophe coming, had lost their positions in the five or ten years before the start of the Khomeini revolution. Left were the yes-men—and the traitors.

The 1976 Amnesty International report put an already vulnerable Shah on the defensive.

It is fairly common knowledge that Amnesty International is a front for British intelligence. At the top are those who know it for certain: Ramsey Clark, Sean McBride, and Conor Cruise O'Brien. An Amnesty adviser, Princeton's Richard Falk, wrote the section of the *1980s Project* devoted to human rights.

Amnesty's 1976 report alleged that the Shah's secret police had tortured and killed political dissidents; its purpose was to foster a climate across the globe in which the Iranian regime was viewed as barbaric and inhuman. Gruesome accounts of electric shock torture and mutilation were played up by the *London Times*, the *Washington Post*, and other respected press. Defending Iranian political prisoners quickly became a *cause célèbre* among radicals and leftists.

The Shah was forced into a position of defending an organization that had no defense. Since its founding in 1955, the secret Savak had been put under the control of British and Israeli intelligence. It tended to act autonomously of the Shah's government; indeed, at times the Savak was in control of the Shah and not the other way around. Most of the agency's torturers had been trained by Israel's Mossad. Its power was increased by occasional acts of terrorism by the left that enabled it to take ruthless repressive action. Many thoughtful Iranians now suspect that the Savak used agent provocateurs to strengthen its hand with the Shah.

Amnesty International soon found that it had powerful friends. With only a few months in office, President Jimmy Carter launched his own "human rights" campaign. Although nominally aimed at violations of human rights by communist countries—excluding the People's Republic of China—the campaign was more often used to keep allies—like Iran—in line. U.S. intelligence officials warned that to apply human rights criterion to the situation, say, of Iran would lead to disaster and would grossly upset legitimate U.S. interests in the Persian Gulf. Such warnings did not deter Zbigniew Brzezinski or Secretary of State Cyrus Vance. The Human Rights Division at State under Patricia Derian soon became one of the most active departments at Foggy Bottom.

Vance's old friend, Deputy Secretary of State Warren Christopher, directed the operation. Christopher had earlier served under the Johnson administration as the No. 2 man at Ramsey Clark's Department of Justice.

After Amnesty's declaration of war, scores of radical and leftist organizations sprang into action against the Shah. CBS-TV's weekly *60 Minutes* produced a broadcast to prove that agents of the Shah's secret police had plotted to kill several Iranian opposition figures, including the man who is now Iran's foreign minister, Sadegh Ghotbzadeh, and a publisher of anti-Shah literature in Virginia. Into full mobilization went the Bertrand Russell Peace Foundation, the Lelio Basso Foundation in Italy, the Institute for Policy Studies in Washington, the Transnational Institute in Amsterdam, the Socialist International machine in Europe, the American Friends

Service Committee, the Libyan-backed Mediterranean People's Congress, and the many human rights organizations such as the International Association of Democratic Jurists. Through these organizations, the radical professors and others shuttled back and forth to Teheran from various Western capitals to make contact with the opposition.

In Iran, there was only one organization of any importance to link up to: the Muslim Brotherhood.

Gathered into the Fedayeen-e Islam were the mullahs led by Ayatollah Khalkhali and Ayatollah Khomeini, who represented the organizing core behind the revolution. Throughout the country, some 200,000 mullahs, positioned in every town and village, followed the dictates of a few fanatics at the head of the Brotherhood. Several dozen of these mullahs and the ayatollahs commanded huge followings.

The other arm of Khomeini's revolution was the coterie of experience, Western-trained, intelligence agents who clustered around the clergy. These are today's surviving secular office-holders: Sadegh Ghotbzadeh, Ibrahim Yazdi, and Abolhassan Bani-Sadr.

Direction from Washington and London came via the "professors," men such as Professor Richard Cottam of the University of Pittsburgh.

Cottam had met Yazdi in Iran as early as the 1950s, when Cottam was a field officer for the CIA attached to the U.S. embassy in Teheran. Cottam also met and guided another member of the future leadership of the Iranian revolution, Ghotbzadeh. For the next twenty years, the Pittsburgh professor joined Yazdi and Ghotbzadeh for strategy sessions in the United States, Europe, and Iran. Yazdi and Cottam were so close that

Yazdi's wife once described Cottam as "a very close friend of my husband, the one person who knows more about him than even I do."

In 1970, Cottam visited Iran again. "Ghotbzadeh set up a lot of contacts for me while I was there," Cottam reminisces. "But he did a sloppy job. I almost blew some covers." In 1977, he made contact with Mohammed Darakhshesh, a radical Iranian who had been a leader many years earlier of the revolt against the Shah's 1963 White Revolution.

In 1977, Darakhshesh traveled to Washington through France. Making contact with the opposition to the Shah, Darakhshesh met in the United States with Cottam, and he asked the Pittsburgh professor to intercede on his behalf with the new Carter administration. Cottam went to Washington and there discussed supporting Khomeini with the U.S. National Security Council.

At about the same time, Yazdi and Ghotbzadeh, looking for funds, were both shuttling back and forth between the United States and France, with visits to Iraq where Khomeini was living in exile. The first money came from the Libyan government of Muammar Qaddafi. A great deal of work needed to be done. Scattered around the world were scores of disorganized centers of Iranian student and other opposition groups. Nearly the entire leadership of Iran under Khomeini would be drawn from these groups, to the exclusion of the Iranians who stayed inside the country to fight the revolution.

Yazdi was the paradigm of such "revolutionaries." He had been constantly at Khomeini's side during the ayatollah's stay outside Paris at Neauphle-le-Château, along with Ghotbzadeh and Bani-Sadr—the inner circle of Khomeini's "Paris advisers." After February 1979, Yazdi was named "deputy prime minister for revolutionary affairs," from which post he helped set up Khomeini's secret police, the Savama. Later, he became foreign minister, resigning in November 1979, after the takeover of the U.S. embassy, only to return to a behind-the-scenes job with Khomeini's inner clique.

Yazdi's first trip to the United States was in 1959. He received a doctorate from the Massachusetts Institute of Technology, and then joined the faculty of Fairleigh Dickinson University. Although he had been implicated in a case involving rape charges and other sex crimes, Yazdi easily obtained status as an American permanent resident—and, eventually, citizenship of the United States—through the aid of New Jersey Senator Harrison Williams.

In 1963, Yazdi worked to found the Muslim Brotherhood's American branch, the "Muslim Student Association." By now a political operative, Yazdi also set up the Iranian Students Association and later the Young Muslims Organization.

In 1964, he left the United States for Europe, spending about three years in France, West Germany, and the American University of Beirut, a bastion of Anglo-American intelligence in the Middle East.

During his three years in Paris, Yazdi worked with Ghotbzadeh and a loose grouping of French anglophiles, existentialists, environmentalists, and anthropologists now lined up behind the Khomeini movement.

Returning to the United States in 1967, he moved to Houston, Texas, taking up a research and training post at Baylor Medical College. "I doubt he did much teaching," commented Georgetown University's Thomas

Ricks, the national coordinator of the People's Committee on Iran. "Every six weeks or so he was always coming to Washington, meeting with all kinds of people, building up his Young Muslims Organizations and so forth. He was always very careful, very discreet, about his meetings."

But during his years away from Iran by far the most important person Yazdi came into contact with was Professor Ali Shariati, the fanatic Iranian ideologue whose notions of "Islamic socialism" supplied the synthetic basis for the Khomeini movements, especially among Iranian students. Shariati was not working alone; he was funded by the Bertrand Russell Peace Foundation. From his position at the University of Mashad he gathered around him a following of zealous revolutionaries among Iranian secondary school and college students. In Paris together in 1964, Yazdi and Shariati discussed returning to Iran together. It was decided that Shariati would go first, to be followed by Yazdi. The guru was captured and arrested on the border entering Iran, and instructed Yazdi not to come.

It took nearly fifteen years for Yazdi to get back to Iran—at the head of the entourage of the Ayatollah Khomeini.

2

How the British
Brought Down
The Shah

It is August 1978. Trouble had been brewing in Iran
for almost a year, with visible revolts beginning in
January 1978 after President Carter's New Year's praise
of Iran as an "island of stability."

The situation had started deteriorating a year earlier
when the Shah had changed prime ministers, replacing
Prime Minister Abbas Amir Hoveyda with Jamshid
Amouzegar. The chief impact of the Amouzegar appointment was to decelerate Iran's development push, orient-
ing investment toward agriculture and away from industry and high-technology sectors.

Amouzegar had also adopted a curious position vis-à-
vis the clergy, carrying out actions that superficially
seemed to be aimed against the mullahs, but that seemed
only to exacerbate the campaign against the government.
Amouzegar had unilaterally suspended payments the

regime had been making to the clergy, causing the first signs of unrest in the mosques. Ill-timed provocations— including insulting letters against the clergy published in the Iranian press by information ministry officials and, in May 1978, a police raid on the home of Iran's leading clergyman, Ayatollah Shareatmadari—fueled the discontent.

The Shah seemed almost oblivious to the simmering volcano beneath him, and he continued to place his trust entirely in the Savak and the security services.

That was his biggest mistake.

The man in charge of Savak's day-to-day affairs was General Hossein Fardoust, a childhood friend of the Shah who had attended the Le Rosey school in Switzerland with him in the 1930s. According to information now available, Fardoust was likely the ringleader of the "inside" track of the revolution; for at least a full year before February 1979 he was carefully exploring for allies among the commanders of the armed forces and the intelligence services. Fardoust would sound out whether a particular officer, perhaps with longstanding grudges against the Shah, would agree to join the Islamic revolution. "The Americans have decided to get rid of the Shah," Fardoust would say. "We have to save ourselves. Will you join us?" Many did.

Both the Shah and his sister Princess Ashraf have said that they consider General Fardoust to have been a traitor to the regime. In her book, *Faces in a Mirror*, Ashraf says that, after the suspension of subsidies to the clergy, the mosques became the scene of often violent anti-Shah demonstrations.

But, she says, "Curiously, Savak, the Shah's secret police—the supposedly all-seeing, all-knowing intelligence source—made no reports on the extent and manner in which the mullahs were now using the sanctity of the pulpit to undermine the throne. . . . Fardoust functioned as a kind of conduit for vital information on the highest level, which he delivered to my brother. . . . I am convinced Fardoust must have withheld vital information from the Shah and was, in fact, in active negotiations with Khomeini during the last years of the regime."

Today, Fardoust is rumored to be one of the leaders of Khomeini's Savama; his home was linked to the December 1979 murder of Prince Shafiq in Paris. Concerning that charge, the Shah told an interviewer after the murder, "In my inner heart I hope it's not true. Because it would be so . . . I mean, dirty, so vile, so disgusting." But in the months leading to February 1979, Fardoust enjoyed the monarch's wholehearted trust.

In early August 1978, Iran was ripped by the worst act of terrorism in history. After a week of scattered violence, over 400 people died on August 19 when a fire raged through the Rex Cinema in Abadan. The fire, it was clear, had been set deliberately, and the doors to the theater barricaded from the outside to prevent any escape from the inferno. Amid mounting tension in Iran and charges of Savak involvement in setting the fire, the official Pars News Service began its own campaign.

"There are two forces responsible for manipulating the current outbreaks—a mass of common naive people who have been subjected to systematic brainwashing are being manipulated by both religious fanaticism and the landed classes," said Pars on August 18. The rioters and terrorists "are encouraged by certain foreign elements which are hostile to the development of Iran," the news service charged.

For several weeks already, the Iranian press had been growing increasingly hostile to the British, and in street discussions most Iranians admitted that the movement led by Khomeini and the mullahs was organized by London.

Special attacks were reserved for the British Broadcasting Corporation (BBC), whose Persian-language broadcasts into Iran fanned the flames of revolt. In late July, the Iranian Workers Organization issued what amounted to an officially sanctioned attack on the BBC: "The BBC has been insulting and criticizing the Iranian nation in its Persian broadcasting services. . . . Iranian development and progress is like a thorn in the eyes of the British imperialists."

So widespread were attacks on the British in Iran that the press in London was compelled to take notice of it. In the August 21 *London Times* former British intelligence officer Lord Chalfont noted with characteristic British understatement: "There are, in Teheran, so many explanations for the current unrest. One school of thought advances the curious proposition of a British conspiracy; however, it turns out, on closer investigation, that no one can provide any evidence or even logical justification for this bizarre theory." Lord Chalfont added that the "Iranian government has traced some of the money back to numbered bank accounts in Switzerland. Here, predictably, the trail goes cold."

The Shiite clergy-led rebellion was also fed by the daily influx of hundreds of thousands of desperate, displaced peasants into Iran's major cities. The migration from the countryside was the fruit of the economic policies of the Amouzegar government, which, by halting many construction and development projects, created instant unemployment among the country's semi-skilled and unskilled labor force. Arriving in the cities, these peasants were shunted right into the mob violence that was gaining new strength with every new action.

The rabble-rousers of the revolution were the mullahs in the mosques. Inviolate to police and law-enforcement authorities, the mosques became rallying points. Speeches by the leading ayatollahs, repeated in hundreds of other speeches throughout the country, whipped up the semiliterate people of Iran to a frenzy, at the end of which they would swarm out onto the streets, chanting and singing praises of the exiled Ayatollah Khomeini.

It was not a political revolution, but a process of cult building, of conditioning the fearful and desperate emotions of Iran's backward peasants into a political battering ram of self-destruction. It was the mass suicide of the Reverend Jim Jones's People's Temple on a national scale. When a group of fanatic marchers, often drugged with opium and told by the mullahs that by dying they would be saved (martyrdom is a centuries-old tradition in Shiism), charged into the gun barrels of poorly trained police, their deaths only triggered further marches. Then, as is the custom among Shiites, on the fortieth day after any death, new ceremonial marches were staged in memory of the dead. The result was new casualties. This forty-day cycle, which began in the spring of 1978, was to repeat itself with quickening intensity throughout the year.

Finally, in the first week of September 1978, after several days of demonstrations bringing millions of Iranians into the street, the Shah acceded to pressure from his generals and declared martial law. That martial law had not been declared many months earlier can be ascribed to one factor only: the clamorous pressure of Amnesty International's "human rights" campaign. Not that the Shah was worried about only Amnesty and its allies; the American and British ambassadors in Teheran quietly had been warning that if the Shah declared martial law, his standing in world opinion would plummet sharply. By hesitating so long in taking a tough stand against the lunatics of the Shiite clergy, the Shah had given them enough rope to begin the cycle of demonstrations and death marches. Now by declaring martial law, he was not only confronting his own countrymen but the U.S. administration and the British. The showdown had begun.

On Friday, September 8, the Shah named General Gholam Ali Oveissi as administrator of martial law. Formerly the commander of the Imperial Guard, the Shah's elite force, Oveissi had a reputation as a hawk. For some reason, the declaration of martial law, though broadcast on the radio, was not heard by many people. Later that day a clash developed between police and demonstrators who had not been told by their leaders that martial law had banned all manifestations. Up to 500 demonstrators were killed in what became known as "Black Friday."

The Shah had thrown down the gauntlet: there was no turning back now. Although he would still seek compromise, compromise was no longer an option, and his hesitation would cost him dearly.

The day after the massacre, the word was out that the White House had decided to get rid of the Shah. French columnist Paul Marie de la Gorce reported: "It was clear, over the last several days, that the calculations of the Shah aiming to reconcile the moderate elements of the Shiite clergy was in the process of failure. From all evidence, the Shah could not wait any longer to impose martial law. He knew very well that his removal was already being openly discussed, including among his longtime allies—the Americans. . . . There were other solutions being prepared in other Washington circles."

From outside Iran, two institutions in particular aided the on-the-ground war against the Shah: British Petroleum and the British Broadcasting Corporation.

It has gone unnoticed that during the entire year of 1978, negotiations were proceeding between the government of Iran and the oil consortium represented by British Petroleum. Talks on renewing the 25-year contract that began in 1953 after the Anglo-American intelligence coup d'état that restored the Shah to the throne, had started in January 1978, and continued through the rest of the year. By October, they collapsed.

Iranians on the inside of the negotiations say that the British were blackmailing Iran during the years preceding the contract's end by refusing to honor an agreement to buy most of Iran's oil production. Although BP and its allies had the authority to purchase up to 8 million barrels of oil per day from Iran by 1978, and had agreed to a minimum of 5 million, they were contracting for only 3 to 4 million. This forced Iran to adjust its income expectations and try to market the oil independently, which they had been doing successfully.

Now, in October 1978, at the height of the revolution, the Shah and the National Iranian Oil Company (NIOC) were negotiating the economic future of Iran.

BP rejected NIOC's demands out of hand, refusing to promise to buy Iranian oil but demanding the exclusive right to buy that oil should it wish to in the future! The Shah and NIOC flatly rejected BP's final offer, and it appeared that if the Shah overcame the revolt, then Iran would be totally free in its oil sales policy in 1979, able to market its own oil to the state companies of France, Spain, Brazil, and many other countries on a state-to-state basis.

"If the consortium [BP] is not willing to show more flexibility in its dealings, perhaps it is time for Iran to reconsider its overall relationship with the companies," declared an editorial in Iran's *Kayhan International* in September. In retrospect, the 25-year partnership with the consortium and the 50-year relationship with British Petroleum which preceded it have not been satisfactory ones for Iran. . . . Looking to the future, NIOC should plan to handle all operations by itself. . . . While this would shift investment obligations wholly onto the NIOC it would simultaneously have the attraction of placing the profitable marketing of all the country's oil products into the hands of the state-owned company. The question on the minds of the oil industry executives here is: has the time for change finally come?"

Almost simultaneously, the first signs of worker unrest began in the Iranian oil fields. Iranian oil output was slowed, several times during 1978, to a trickle. In the middle of the Iran-BP negotiations, Iran's chief asset—its enormous oil wealth—was suddenly eliminated as a chip for bargaining.

Iran's oil workers, according to reports, were organized primarily by a team of radicals sent into Khuzestan by the Bertrand Russell Peace Foundation.

In the American press, not a single line was published

about the Iranian fight with BP during the entire revolutionary period.

Simultaneously, capital began leaving the country— a flight organized through BP channels among Iran's financial elite. This elite, represented primarily in certain Bahai cult, Jewish, and other bankers and merchants, had family connections to the British merchants and BP dating back to the nineteenth century.

On the lower levels, this alliance rested on the historic agreements between the Shiite leadership and the underworld of the bazaar merchants. Dependent on financing at high rates of interest, the *bazaaris* had struck political and economic deals of convenience with the merchant banks.

The bazaaris were traditionally connected to the unregulated monetary flows and smuggling within the Arab littoral states in the Persian Gulf. Exerting tremendous power over this uncontrolled financial nexus are a number of prominent and financially powerful Jewish families. Known as the "Jewish rug merchants," these financial concerns have the ability to exert an impact on Iran's economy through massive capital flight amounting to tens of millions of dollars within hours. The *New York Post* reported in October 1978 that in that month alone over $700 million left Iran through channels controlled by the Iranian Jewish community.

None of this could have occurred without a green light from the British, whose intelligence service watches the goings-on in the Persian Gulf markets with extreme care. For two centuries the British have controlled the smuggling and drug trade in the Gulf as a way station between Asia's Far East Golden Triangle and the West. Through these channels, vast amounts of arms and ammunition were smuggled into Iran to feed the rebellion—and money was smuggled out.

It was in this period, between late September and the beginning of November, that the Shah missed his last real opportunity to stem the tide.

By October, the Iranian nation was well aware that the British-sponsored clergy was determined to bring down the regime. It was the talk of Teheran. Had the Shah taken the decision to confront the British openly and directly, he could have defeated them. That strategy would have centered around the Shah's launching his *own* revolution, by declaring that the security of Iran was threatened by a British imperialist conspiracy and by British Petroleum. He would have been able to paint the clergy as "black reactionaries" in the service of London, and rallied most of Iran's political elite to his side. As it was, his poor political administration had propelled many of the middle class and intellectuals to the side of the fanatic Khomeini in the hope of latching their fortunes onto the mullahs' revolution.

In the international domain, conditions were ripe for the Shah to pull a political coup against the British: If he had suddenly decided to nationalize BP and the rest of the consortium and market all of Iranian oil independently, breaking the expiring agreement, there were signs that France, West Germany, and Japan would have ignored any British calls for a boycott (as happened in 1951, under Mossadegh) and reached state-to-state deals with Iran.

The Soviet Union and its allies were also prepared to support the Shah against Khomeini. In late October, the Shah had received birthday telegrams from Leonid I. Brezhnev of the Soviet Union and many Eastern European leaders. Brezhnev's message had called for an expansion of relations between the Soviet Union and its neighbor, economically and politically. In 1978, a Tass release from Moscow urgently denied reports from Anglo-American sources that Moscow was behind the unrest in Iran and declared, "In order to uncover the reasons for the present disturbances in Iran, the CIA Director would have to look particularly at the policy of his own country." Tass called charges by CIA Director Stansfield Turner about a Soviet role in fomenting unrest in Iran a "propagandistic coverup for the American secret services in Teheran."

Neighboring Iraq, which had watched Khomeini's opposition to the Shah carefully, took action on September 27. The ayatollah was placed under arrest in Najaf, the Iraqi holy city. Not only Iraq, but many Arab states were prepared to support the Shah against the clergy, whose revolution, they feared, would later spread into the Arab world.

But the Shah did not act.

Without the British Broadcasting Corporation, there would have been no Khomeini. During the entire year of 1978, the BBC stationed dozens of correspondents throughout the country, in every remote town and village. BBC correspondents, often part-time stringers for Khomeini, sometimes full-time British nationals in the employ of the British secret service, worked as the intelligence service for the revolution.

As soon as a small incident occurred in some village, the BBC correspondent on the scene would relay the news to BBC headquarters in Teheran. Within hours,

BBC Persian-language broadcasts would beam exaggerated accounts of the incident to all Iran! Functioning as the national loudspeaker for the mullahs and their sympathizers, each day the BBC would beam into Iran gory accounts of alleged atrocities committed by the Iranian police—often without checking the veracity of the report. The Iranian government was never given a chance to rebut. Propagandists like Ibrahim Yazdi were given hours of air time to vent their spleen against the Shah, all of which was eagerly listened to by the Shah's enemies in Iran.

By late fall, the BBC was broadcasting the long, ranting speeches of the lunatic Ayatollah Khomeini himself—in their entirety. Several times during November and December, the Shah said he would take reprisal against London if the BBC's subversion were not halted. Once he threatened to break diplomatic relations with Great Britain. But the British government solemnly swore it had no influence over the BBC which, they claimed, was a "private corporation." At least twice the Shah summoned the British ambassador in Teheran to protest the actions of the BBC, but to no avail. From time to time, the government would expel a BBC correspondent, but no more.

Not until November 30, 1978, did a member of the Iranian Parliament, Hossein Daneshi from Abadan, demand to know why the BBC had been permitted to play its provocateur role: "A glance at the events and developments throughout the world over the past year demonstrates a diabolical plan aimed at the disintegration of Iran. . . . You should not be surprised if you see that the BBC prepares programs and during its three programs in Persian thinks of nothing but to make provocations, create disturbances, and chaos. This old fox Britain, no longer able to secure good for itself, is looking for a prey.

"My question for the government is this," declared Daneshi. "Why does it not clarify political facts and why does it not inform the people about political developments in the world which have been launched against Iran? Why does the government not unveil Britain's design as it is still tasting the fruits of its plunderings?"

Why indeed? With the gathering storm, the BBC became the de facto coordinator for revolution. On less than twenty-four hours notice, Teheran's mullahs could organize simultaneous demonstrations in Iranian cities separated by a thousand miles—through the BBC. In Paris, Khomeini made tapes ordering his cult followers to rampage through the streets. Within hours, his precise instructions, in his own voice in Persian, would be broadcast into Iran from BBC's London headquarters.

Belying its origins as an arm of the British Special Operations Executive, the BBC began to broadcast psywar rumors in December, such as reports claiming that the Shah had fled the country, or had abdicated the throne to his son, or had gone insane. In December the Iranian Information Minister Tehrani accused the BBC of inciting the Iranian oil workers to strike. A BBC United Press International correspondent was expelled for reporting that the Shah had been assassinated. For a brief time that month, as the *Washington Post* reported that the BBC was considered to be Iran's "Public Enemy No. 1," the military government of Prime Minister General Gholam Reza Azhari jammed the BBC broadcasts. It was too late.

The Shah's enemies in the clergy were not averse to a little psychological warfare of their own. Once, during a scheduled demonstration in Teheran on December 2, 1978, when the violence that antigovernment fanatics hoped for did not materialize, the Shiite clergy brought professionally made tape recordings of screams, gunshots, and violence and played them over loudspeakers from the minarets of the mosques! Within hours, BBC correspondents in "on the scene" newscasts had their accounts of the December 2 demonstrations beaming into Irán, complete with background noise courtesy of the mullahs' electronic equipment. The next day, people emerging from their homes found red stains on the pavement where the march had taken place; the mullahs had poured red-colored dye on the streets to simulate blood.

Tactics like this, everyone knew, so highly effective with Iran's population, were not devised by illiterate mullahs.

By this time, in Washington, the final go-ahead had been given to replace the Shah with the ayatollah. In November, the Carter administration announced that it had appointed George Ball of the Trilateral Commission and the Bilderberg Society to head a special NSC task force on Iran and the Persian Gulf. Ball, who had long been known as an anti-Shah advocate of the human-rights mafia's views, delivered the obituary-in-advance for the Pahlavi regime, recommending that the United States drop its support of the Shah and make contacts with the opposition.

In early January 1979, at a meeting of the heads of state of the United States, Great Britain, France, and West Germany in Guadeloupe, the U.S. administration formally announced to its allies that it would no longer work to keep the Shah in power. With the "Islamic card" now on the table, it was only a matter of time before the Shah was ousted.

Reflecting on the process of events that destroyed his regime, the Shah of Iran wrote later in his memoirs, *Answer to History:* "I did not know it then—perhaps I did not want to know—but it is clear to me now that the Americans wanted me out. Certainly this is what the human rights advocates in the State Department wanted, and Secretary Vance apparently acceded. I say apparently because I was never told anything: nothing about the split in the Carter administration over Iran policy; nothing about the hopes some American officials put in the viability of an 'Islamic Republic' as a bulwark against communist incursions.

"What was I to make, for example, of the administration's sudden decision to call former Under Secretary of State George Ball to the White House as an adviser on Iran? I knew that Ball was no friend and I understood that he was working on a special report concerning Iran. No one ever informed me what areas the report was to cover, let alone its conclusions. I read them months later in exile and found my worst fears confirmed. Ball was among those Americans who wanted to abandon me and ultimately my country."

At this point, France's role became crucial. The French and the West Germans were well aware that a Khomeini regime would seriously destabilize the Persian Gulf and threaten their oil supply. They also knew that, using Khomeini as an excuse, the U.S. military would begin pressing for an expanded presence in the Indian Ocean area, which could upset the balance of world strategic forces and, in the opinion of Paris and Bonn, lead to World War III. Khomeini, in the French view, was a highly unstable card to play, one that could trigger the disintegration of the entire Middle East.

France had already made one blunder that President Giscard d'Estaing must have regretted. When Iraq placed the mad ayatollah under arrest in Najaf, the French inexplicably granted Khomeini asylum in France. Reportedly, the French decision was taken under the advice of the Shah, who told Giscard that Paris might better be able to control Khomeini's actions if he were located nearby rather than in some Arab country like Libya. For whatever reason, partly self-serving, the French government allowed Khomeini to arrive, and he took up residence at Neauphle-le-Château near Paris.

The ayatollah became an overnight world celebrity— this was in October 1978—and gave daily interviews to the international press. The French had not calculated on the effect of the electronic media.

A steady stream of American and British agents filed through Khomeini's chateau to make the final arrangements for the transfer of power to the ayatollah. Among Khomeini's guests were Ramsey Clark, the former U.S. attorney general; Joseph Malone, an ex-CIA station chief in Beirut with close ties to British intelligence; Zygmunt Nagorski, a member of the Council on Foreign Relations in New York; and many more.

The Anglo-American scenario for disintegrating the Middle East looked unstoppable. But the French and their allies sought the last chance. On January 6, the Shah had named Shahpour Bakhtiar, a respected member of the National Front, as prime minister.

The Bakhtiar government was the last hope of averting chaos in Iran. Dr. Bakhtiar himself had close ties to France and was held in high esteem among Iranian nationalists. He had been jailed under the Shah for his role among the democratic opposition, but he had no connections to a reactionary clergy. During World War II, he fought in the Free French armed forces against the Nazis, and his son is today a serving member of the French intelligence service. It was now Bakhtiar's responsibility to organize a national consensus around sanity to prevent power from slipping into the hands of the Dark Ages mullahs. No one could consider him a puppet of the Shah; if he could pull together a government, then perhaps Khomeini could be stopped.

The French, and their continental West European allies, were willing to help.

"When, in 1940, Charles de Gaulle climbed into his modest plane to go to London, he was not convinced of success either," declared Bakhtiar in an interview just after he formed his cabinet.

Some two weeks earlier, Bakhtiar had joined forces with Darious Farouhar, another member of the National Front, the main nonclergy opposition group that had been founded by Mohammed Mossadegh in the 1940s. Farouhar was called upon to back the effort of Prime Minister Siddighi to form a cabinet in late January. That effort failed, and so Bakhtiar took the mantle. On January 3, in the United States, Lyndon LaRouche urged the world's governments to throw all of their support behind Bakhtiar's effort to form a constitutional government.

In the five weeks that Bakhtiar served as prime minister, he displayed enormous courage and resolve to prevent Iran from falling into the Khomeini abyss. For his efforts, he was "expelled" from the National Front by its chairman, Karim Sanjabi, an opportunistic fool who decided early on that Bakhtiar could not succeed and instead traveled to Paris where he signed a pact with Khomeini. (For his reward, Sanjabi later served briefly as Khomeini's first foreign minister, until he was forced out of office and replaced by Yazdi.) Bakhtiar laughed at Sanjabi's mistakes, urging him to come back into the fold and break with Khomeini. "If Karim Sanjabi, who has just excluded me in a somewhat ridiculous fashion from the National Front, accepts the post as president of the regency council, the place awaits him." But Sanjabi would not accept.

Bakhtiar also sought an agreement with the Shah concerning control of the armed forces. Reluctant to give Bakhtiar full military control, the Shah demanded to retain the figurehead title of commander-in-chief. To strengthen his position with the armed forces, Bakhtiar asked General Feredoun Djam, a former chief of staff who had had a falling out with the Shah years earlier, to return to Iran as his defense minister. Djam was highly respected by the armed forces, and would help Bakhtiar rally their support.

As soon as his government was ratified by the parliament, Bakhtiar began pushing through a series of major reform acts. Among them, he completely nationalized all British oil interests and concessions in Iran; put an end to martial law; abolished the secret police, Savak; pulled Iran out of the Central Treaty Organization and declared that Iran would no longer be "the gendarme of the Gulf." He also announced that he was removing Ardeshir Zahedi from his position as Iran's ambassador to the United States.

The Zahedi story is curious. Although Zahedi was assigned to Washington as the Shah's envoy, for the last several months before the revolution he had returned to Teheran, where he could be found at the Shah's constant side. Many, including Iran's former ambassador to the United Nations, Feredoun Hoveyda, have hinted that Zahedi was part of the Khomeini conspiracy and was using his position to misinform the Shah. Whether the Shah trusted him is unclear; what is certain is that every day, and sometimes twice a day, Zahedi would speak by telephone with Zbigniew Brzezinski in Washington. Through Zahedi came Brzezinski's marching orders for the besieged monarch.

David Aaron, Brzezinski's closest aide, was meanwhile putting together an Iran Task Force that included close consultation with the pro-Khomeini "Iran experts" such as Marvin Zonis, Richard Cottam, James Bill, and so forth. Aaron also served as liaison with the State Department's Warren Christopher and with Ramsey Clark, Christopher's former boss.

Bakhtiar faced two sorts of opposition. On the one hand, the clergy and the radical-leftist backers of the Khomeini forces were constantly agitating against Bakhtiar; on the other hand, the conservative military, which was absolutely loyal to the Shah, was threatening a military coup against Bakhtiar in support of the Shah. The generals, politically naive and unable to believe that the United States government was supporting Khomeini, steadfastly waited for orders from the Shah and "the Americans" to make a coup—orders that never came. Others waited to move with Khomeini.

Bakhtiar was conducting round-the-clock negotiations to find a workable coalition to support his regime, and until the last minute, there were chances he might succeed. The respected Ayatollah Shareatmadari showed

The joint general staff and the command of the entire Iranian armed forces met to discuss the crisis. Then in a shock to the world, they emerged to declare that the Imperial Armed Forces would remain "impartial" in the crisis! The declaration appeared over the signature of the Iranian Chief of Staff, General Gharabaghi.

That decision was imposed with brutal force. Its very issuance meant that the armed forces had withdrawn from the battle, and the troops were ordered to pull back into their barracks. Teheran and Iran's other cities were handed over to the mobs of Khomeini worshippers. Resistance to the army's decision was met with summary execution. A group around General Abdul Ali Badri and his associates opposed Gharabaghi's edict and began making plans for a coup against the Khomeini forces to preserve order—when he and his allies were shot in cold blood by officers following Gharabaghi's command!

All across Teheran, dozens of other officers were shot by hit teams under Gharabaghi and General Fardoust's control.

Another defector was Air Force commander General Hossein Rabii. Although Rabii had earned a reputation as a hardline loyalist to the Shah, in the crucial hours of February 9-11, he suddenly announced that he was switching sides and "joining the revolution." Reportedly, General Rabii had been promised his own survival and help to leave the country, in exchange for his cooperation in securing the airports and fields for Khomeini. Soon afterwards, Rabii was doublecrossed, arrested, and machine-gunned to death a few minutes after a kangaroo-court trial.

In the next forty-eight hours, up to 350 Iranian

officers of the top command were murdered by professional assassin teams. Their names were apparently printed out from a computer at military headquarters, which revealed every man in a command position of logistical control, communications, and mobile units. Those who refused to cooperate with the "revolution" were eliminated.

Professionals in the military field were amazed at how easily the 350,000-man Iranian armed forces were paralyzed and disintegrated. Repeatedly, in this connection, one name comes up: General Robert E. Huyser of the United States Air Force.

Then serving as the No. 2 man in the NATO Command in Brussels under Alexander Haig, Huyser was sent to Iran in the beginning of January, a few days before the Guadeloupe meeting at which Carter told the West Germans and French that the United States was dumping the Shah. The visit was scheduled to last only three days, but Huyser stayed in Iran until early February, more than one month after his arrival.

From January 3 to February 4, General Huyser met with the leading generals of the armed forces command every day. The pressure was building in Iran: on January 16, the Shah of Iran left the country on "vacation"— never to return. The army was restive and disoriented, with its commander in chief out of the country. The Shah went to Egypt and then Morocco, and in both places the military leadership reportedly called the Shah and begged him for orders to move against Khomeini. The Shah refused to give the orders. (Later, he would say that he was waiting for permission from Washington to confront Khomeini directly, a remark that disgusted many Iranians who took it to mean that the Shah was openly admitting, finally, that he was a puppet of Washington.)

General Huyser, in constant contact with Brzezinski, told the generals that they must not move militarily against Khomeini, no matter what might happen. If they did, Huyser said, the U.S. military would disown them, halt all supplies of arms and spare parts, and "cut them off at the legs."

Huyser foiled not one but several attempted coups d'etat. His main function was to assure the generals that, when the moment came and the civilian government was incapable of withstanding the revolutionary forces, then the United States would support a military takeover of Iran. Contented with that assurance, many generals simply sat back and waited, and when the mob, armed, took to the streets, did nothing.

"Huyser really worked on them," said a source cited by the *Washington Post*, referring to Iran's command. "He really did a number on them." Said one Iranian general of General Khosrowdad, reportedly one of the coup plotters, "I saw Khosrowdad's face when he came out of one of the briefings. He looked like a private." He was later executed by one of Khomeini's gangs.

To some of the generals, Huyser reportedly stated that the United States did not believe that the Shah could return, and that the Carter administration was seeking a partnership between the clergy and the military. General Gharabaghi may have encouraged this belief with his advocacy of negotiations with the Khomeini camp.

One thing is certain: without General Huyser's mission, Khomeini would not have come to power so effortlessly. The nation of Iran would have faced a bloodbath of extremely serious dimensions, possibly civil war. In the end, many Iranians and other analysts believe, the most extreme forces in the Khomeini camp would have been defeated and moderates forced to compromise, possibly along the lines of the accord that had already been worked out between Bakhtiar and Bazargan. According to former high-ranking Iranian officers, Khomeini would have been instantly assassinated by the army intelligence division, and his followers disorganized.

That never happened. Instead, of the nineteen to twenty Iranian generals who signed the neutrality declaration of February 9, at least ten were shot by Khomeini's Savama and the Revolutionary Guard in the weeks after the revolution; several others are still in prison in Iran. Only a few survived: Fardoust, said to be the chief of Savama under Khomeini; Gharabaghi, who until the summer of 1980 played an important role inside Iran with Khomeini's armed forces; Admiral Kamal Habibollahi, who fled Iran some months after the revolution but reportedly maintained contact with Khomeini's military from the United States; and General Toufanian, now living underground in the United States.

The rest are dead.

General Huyser, reassigned to the Scott Air Force Base in Illinois, where he heads the Military Airlift Command, has not fully explained his mission to anyone.

The best assessment of the Khomeini regime was provided by Prime Minister Bakhtiar several days before the mob swept away his authority. "Khomeini is an ignoramus. He is a jealous, negative, destructive man. Khomeini's entourage is a true zoo comprised of shady and dubious people. Half of the people who are out shouting against me are illiterate, and instead of going to the mosque they should be going to school. What Khomeini has done in a few weeks has already caused more damage than twenty-five years of the Shah's regime."

But what Khomeini would do in the next few months would truly stun the world.

3

Treason In Washington

Between November 1979 and April 1980, the entire world was preoccupied on a day-to-day basis with one question: the taking hostage of fifty-three American citizens by an Iranian mob in Teheran. Not a single government in the world took any decision of consequence during those five months without carefully considering the latest reports on Teheran—from the Soviet Union and Western Europe to the Arab world, Japan, and leading developing nations. As the situation continued to deteriorate, a dozen political leaderships across the globe were paralyzed and began to make preparations for confrontation and possibly World War III; as things improved slightly, they would make cautious explorations toward initiatives in other fields that had been long postponed. Everything hung on the U.S.-Iran "crisis." It was a perfect exercise in global crisis management.

Of all the world's governments, the one the least surprised by the taking of American hostages was the United States government itself. The seizure of the U.S. embassy had taken place with the full knowledge and support of the Carter administration. Khomeini's aggression had the potential to develop into exactly the showdown that would give the Anglo-Americans the opportunity to clobber Western Europe and Japan. The Carter administration's alliance with the Muslim Brotherhood had not ended with the successful completion of General Huyser's mission; nor would it cease with the taking of the American corps.

After Khomeini's seizure of power, the United States did not interrupt its ongoing program of military supply, training, and arms sales to Iran. As the ayatollah ranted and raved against the United States, which he called "the great Satan," Washington was shipping enormous quantities of arms to Khomeini's Guard. Hercules and Boeing 747 air transport aircraft shuttled back and forth between New York and Iran, stopping in Madrid, Spain, and the Azores, carrying spare parts for Iran's American-made helicopters and military aircraft. The equipment was badly needed in the battle to put down Kurdish tribesmen in Iran's western provinces.

This resupply was officially admitted by the State Department and reported at the time in the *Executive Intelligence Review*, the *Wall Street Journal*, the *Financial Times* of London, and elsewhere.

Beginning in the late summer of 1979, U.S. intelligence personnel began to move into Iran to take up positions as advisers to the Iranian secret service, the Savama. According to CIA sources, the American intelligence community had been involved even before the revolution in military training for Khomeini's partisans. The relationship continued after the revolution's success.

David Aaron of the National Security Council, working with Warren Christopher and Ramsey Clark, had put together a team of sixty CIA agents who entered Iran in January 1979, at the same time as General Robert Huyser, to help smooth the transition to Khomeini.

From the Iranian side, the shadowy figure who acted as the overseer of the construction of Iran's Revolutionary Guard and of the dismantling of the huge armed forces was Mustafa Chamran, like Yazdi, a U.S.-trained adviser to Khomeini.

Military advice and provision of supplies are one thing; complicity in the taking of American diplomatic personnel is another. It is difficult to believe that U.S. officials in responsible positions of leadership would so recklessly place Americans' lives—and world peace—in such grave danger to effect a political strategem.

But consider the following: by September 1979 it had become clear that France, West Germany, and their allies did not intend to capitulate to Anglo-American pressure and were proceeding full-steam ahead with the European Monetary System. Despite undisguised threats and blackmail from London and Washington, Western Europe had issued its own declaration of independence and was busily pulling together a coalition that included the Arab world, other OPEC countries, India, Mexico, and the Soviet Union around a strategy whose slogan was, in practice: Peace through Development.

By creating an artificial crisis in Iran, the Carter

administration believed that it could use the international shock created, to go to its allies and demand that they subordinate their independent will to the broader concerns of "the NATO alliance." With American naval vessels steaming toward the Indian Ocean and elite U.S. Air Force units on alert, with the President of the United States threatening to trigger a world war by sending troops into Iran, with two thirds of world oil exports now hanging by a thread in an unstable Persian Gulf, how could the Europeans refuse to submit to the will of the alliance's senior partner, reasoned Washington. Since coming to power in 1977, the Carter administration had sought justification for sending U.S. Marines to seize the oil fields of Saudi Arabia and the Gulf. Finally, with the taking of American hostages, it had a "Reichstag fire."

It is likely that the plan to seize the U.S. embassy received its final approval, making related contingency plans operational, sometime in late September 1979. It was then that Mustafa Chamran, the Berkeley-trained chief of Iran's secret police, was named Iran's defense minister.

In the same month, Iranian moderates, such as Hassan Nazih, who headed the National Iranian Oil Company, were purged from what became a streamlined regime now almost totally under the control of the inner councils of the secretive Muslim Brotherhood.

Chamran's colleague and partner, Foreign Minister Ibrahim Yazdi, was at the time in New York to attend the session of the United Nations General Assembly. Yazdi, who had adopted the studied guise of a Muslim revolutionary ideologue, stalked through the U.N. halls basking in his self-styled reputation as a fiery radical and enemy of "the great Satan," America.

However, in between his revolutionary speechifying at the U.N., Yazdi found time on October 3 to pay a cordial visit to the New York Council on Foreign Relations, where he delivered a speech and then met privately with CFR officials for a period of several hours.

The next day, Yazdi held a closed-door meeting with Secretary of State Cyrus Vance. The *Financial Times* of London reported then on October 5 that, as a result of these meetings, Washington had ordered the "resumption of large-scale airlifts of arms to Iran" and was considering dispatching a "limited number of technicians" to Iran as well. In Iran, Defense Minister Chamran explained that Iran was seeking "foreign advisers" to help train the army and the Revolutionary Guard.

Also from October 3-5, the United States began to strengthen its military presence in the Persian Gulf and the Indian Ocean. The Pentagon announced on October 3 that it was bolstering the U.S. Indian Ocean deployment. On the same day Sultan Qabus of Oman, a British-trained puppet, expressed his country's willingness to have U.S. bases on its soil to "protect" the sea lanes of the Gulf. Immediately, in an unusual interview, Yazdi hinted that Iran might well consider forming an alliance with Oman to protect the straits! Yazdi said that he was "not acquainted with" any plans by Oman already in that direction, but, he added coyly, Iran's "willingness to cooperate" with Oman in the Gulf would "depend on the circumstances." He refused to comment further.

Washington was tightening its cooperation with revolutionary Iran.

During the same few days in the beginning of October, Yazdi made contact with his old friend, Ramsey Clark. A few days later, on October 12, the former U.S.

attorney general sent a letter of crucial significance to the Iranian foreign minister. The letter concerned the ongoing efforts of David Rockefeller and Dr. Henry Kissinger to gain admission for the Shah into the United States for medical treatment.

Clark advised Yazdi: "It is critically important to show that despots cannot escape and live in wealth while nations they ravaged continue to suffer. [I urge] the new government of Iran to seek damages for criminal and wrongful acts committed by the former Shah, and to recover properties from the Shah, his family, and confederates, unlawfully taken from the Iranian people."

The Clark letter was not leaked to the press until after the U.S. embassy was seized on November 4. It was taken as evidence that Special Envoy Clark had incited the Iranians to take over the embassy and demand the return of the Shah to Iran.

On October 14, two days after the Clark letter was written, Yazdi left New York and arrived in Paris to map out an "international campaign" among Iran's ambassadors and intelligence agents to prepare for worldwide agitation on the issue of the return of the Shah to Iran.

Approximately one week later, the State Department announced that it would allow the deposed Shah to come to New York for medical treatment.

The State Department had taken its decision only under pressure of the most extreme sort from Kissinger, the Rockefeller family, and related interests. The Shah was permitted to come to New York despite official advice from the CIA, the U.S. embassy in Teheran, and other sources that his entry would produce a violent reaction in Iran and probably would result in the taking of American hostages.

Official State Department cables released by Representative George Hansen (R-Idaho), dated beginning in August 1979 and continuing through late October, declared repeatedly that the Iranians would probably attempt to storm the embassy if the Shah were allowed into the United States.

A November 18 story in *The New York Times* reported: "The decision was made despite the fact that Mr. Carter and his senior policy advisers had known for months that to admit the Shah would endanger Americans at the embassy in Teheran. An aide reported that at one meeting Mr. Carter had asked, 'When the Iranians take our people in Teheran hostage, what will you advise me then?' "

The *Times* continued: "The Administration was warned repeatedly by the Central Intelligence Agency that the Shah's presence in America might provide the excuse for sharp anti-Americanism and a probable action against the embassy, reminiscent of a one day takeover on Feb. 14."

Immediately after the Shah's October 22 arrival in New York, Iran began making extreme threats against the Carter administration, beginning with protests by oil workers and culminating in an hours' long speech by Ayatollah Khomeini himself on October 29. Khomeini declared that Iran must "shut the door on the West" and ranted, "These American-loving brains must be purged from the country." Finally, on November 1, he called upon Iran's students to "expand with all their might their attacks against the United States and Israel, so they may force the United States to return the deposed and cruel Shah."

Despite such accumulated evidence, not a single additional precaution was taken to protect the embassy!

The Iranian student mob seized the embassy in Iran on November 4. Three days earlier, in Algeria, Zbigniew Brzezinski had held a surprising meeting with Foreign Minister Ibrahim Yazdi. According to intelligence sources, it was during this last tête-à-tête that final details concerning the embassy takeover were hammered out.

Returning to Iran, Yazdi went directly into a meeting with U.S. Chargé d'Affaires Bruce Laingen. During the hours of the embassy seizure, Yazdi and Laingen were meeting together inside the offices of the Iranian foreign ministry. Now, though nominally a hostage, Bruce Laingen is still inside Yazdi's old offices at the foreign ministry, where he has access to a telex machine and other communications facilities. Reportedly, Laingen is a close associate of the Muslim Brotherhood, dating back to his days as the American ambassador to Malta, one of the area headquarters of the Muslim Brotherhood, especially in Libya.

In the next days, President Carter named Ramsey Clark as official White House envoy plenipotentiary to Iran—the same Ramsey Clark who, only a few months earlier, was marching under "Death to America" banners in Teheran.

With the taking of the hostages, the Carter administration—as preplanned—set into motion its scenario for global crisis management.

First, President Carter announced the freezing of all Iranian financial assets in the United States and its banks, including branches of American banks abroad.

Instantly, the world financial markets were thrown into a panic, and big dollar depositors in Western Europe and the United States—particularly the OPEC central banks—began to pull back from further commitments.

The administration had announced that it was invoking the International Emergency Economic Powers Act. The decision, it was learned, had been made two weeks before the embassy was taken over.

Randy Kau, the Federal Emergency Management Agency official placed in the Treasury Department told the *Executive Intelligence Review:* "FEMA is involved in the overall planning. . . . We at FEMA had this plan to freeze the Iranian assets two weeks before we did it, and I spent the entire two weeks on the phone trying to kill the rumors that we would do it."

The admission shows that the Anglo-American financial elite had known that a U.S.-Iran crisis would erupt in November and had already taken measures to protect itself. Among those bankers was David Rockefeller, whose insistent demand that the Shah come to the United States had been the chief cause of the crisis in the first place.

(Somewhat later, Mexican doctors who had been treating the Shah in Mexico angrily revealed that there was absolutely no medical reason why the Shah could not have continued to receive adequate medical care without traveling to the United States.)

The seizure of the $6 billion or more in Iranian U.S. assets had the effect of undermining confidence in the dollar and weakening its value as an international reserve currency. The Eurodollar market was paralyzed, and most international lending halted until complex legal matters were sorted out. In certain respects, the Carter-

U.S. Treasury decision was illegal, since it affected branches of U.S. banks overseas that under normal international law fall under the sovereignty of their host country.

But the most serious result by far was the effect of the Treasury action in scaring other OPEC governments away from any long-term lending, precisely at a time when West Germany and France were seeking to attract such deposits into the financial apparatus associated with the European Monetary System. Only one month before the Iranian crisis erupted, French Foreign Minister Jean François-Poncet had told a United Nations press conference that it was his "vision" that the EMS eventually replace the International Monetary Fund and World Bank as the center of world finance.

The Carter administration's insistent demands that Western Europe and Japan invoke economic sanctions against Iran were like asking its allies to cut their own throats. But the demand succeeded in raising tensions between the Europeans and the oil-producing countries, including Saudi Arabia, which saw the possibility of economic confrontation between the developed West and OPEC as a grave threat to its own interests.

Second, the U.S.-Iranian confrontation gave Carter the pretext he sought for vastly expanding U.S. military presence in the Middle East and the Indian Ocean. Within days of the taking of the hostages, a U.S. fleet of several aircraft carriers and up to thirty other vessels was dispatched to the Gulf; the U.S. naval presence in nearby waters was reinforced; and negotiations were opened for U.S. military facilities in the Indian Ocean littoral states of Oman, Somalia, and Kenya.

Contingency plans for building up U.S. military

forces in Egypt, with related support from Israel, became operational. Heavy pressure was placed on Saudi Arabia and other states in the region to join the American military effort, and the Camp David axis took on renewed vigor as a tool of NATO influence in the Middle East.

These measures were not aimed at the Iranians.

At any moment, the Pentagon might order a sudden military strike against Iran, in the form of a seizure of Iran's Kharg Island, from which oil exports are loaded; or a bombing of Iran's oil fields; or a naval blockade of the Persian Gulf; or even a desperate effort to rescue the hostages. Any one or all of these measures would not dissuade Khomeini.

Instead, as most analysts acknowledged at the time, the chief effect of any U.S. military action would be to create an uncontrollable situation near the source of two thirds of the world's oil supplies and probably trigger an outbreak of radical terrorism throughout the Arabian Gulf states by the Muslim Brotherhood.

Washington had neatly positioned itself into a situation in which it could almost dictate its demands to Western Europe and Japan. "Go along with what we say, or we will cut off your oil supplies," was the message delivered to European capitals from the Carter administration.

The message was not lost on the European elite. In a November 28 column in *Le Figaro*, Paul Marie de la Gorce—whose columns often reflect views of the French presidential palace—examined the options under discussion for U.S. military action against Iran and concluded that each of them would mean "more damages for Europe and Japan than for Iran." Those who advocate such solutions, he said, are "consciously or not inspired by the lessons given by Henry Kissinger," and he warned that even world war could result from such a clumsy intervention.

The crisis simmered for several months on the brink of confrontation. Throughout the winter President Carter's reelection chances shot up so rapidly that Ted Kennedy's head spun, and Carter played the hostage crisis for all it was worth. On the eve of the crucial New Hampshire primary, for instance, the President let it be known that a diplomatic initiative involving the United Nations and Iran's newly elected President, Bani-Sadr, was about to secure the release of the hostages—but, of course, no such release took place.

Finally, at the end of April, the Iran crisis broke in a way that almost touched off World War III.

The April 24 American military rescue operation into Iran was a hoax. But it was a hoax that came within inches of enveloping the United States in a thermonuclear holocaust.

That the raid would occur was no secret. Professionals in the world's intelligence community expected the American armed forces to attempt a rescue mission or retaliatory action. In its April 22 issue, the *Executive Intelligence Review* reported—in an article written at least six days before the April 24 raid—that the Carter administration "has begun a headlong drive toward a 'Cuban missile crisis'-style thermonuclear confrontation with the Soviet Union over Iran, timed to occur between late April and May 11, for the purposes of blackmailing Western Europe and Japan into submitting to Anglo-American political dictates."

European statesmen were told bluntly that Carter

and Brzezinski would view the response of Europe to the Iran intervention as a "test of the Atlantic alliance." According to sources in Paris and Bonn, Western Europe pointed out that any unilateral military action by Washington would not only result in a strategic disaster, but probably would lead to Soviet intervention in Iran.

To this, Brzezinski replied curtly that "it is now up to Europe to prevent World War III," reported the West German *Frankfurter Rundschau*.

The Soviet Union was equally explicit in its warnings. "Washington is not only aiming at aggravating its conflict with Teheran," said *Pravda* April 11. "Judging from everything it is venturing a risky bluff: blackmailing Iran, as well as America's allies who depend on oil deliveries from the Persian Gulf, with the threat of direct military intervention." This strategy, said *Pravda*, "puts Western Europe and Japan in the position of being forced participants in a game designed to strengthen the shaken position of U.S. imperialism in the Near and Middle East." *Pravda* concluded that "the prospect of being deprived of Iranian oil does not provoke any enthusiasm, especially not in Tokyo, Bonn, or Paris."

And, just before the U.S. intervention, Zbigniew Brzezinski himself declared that the Soviet Union was building up its military for a possible intervention. "There are reports, credible reports, of a Soviet build-up in the Transcaucasian Military District in some patterns reminiscent of the Soviet build-up north of Afghanistan," he stated.

Yet, despite the risk of World War III, President Carter in mid-April delivered a terrifying ultimatum to Western Europe. "I expect them to comply with the political and economic sanctions against Iran," declared

Carter, or else the U.S. response "may well involve military means." That same day, Deputy Secretary of State Warren Christopher told ABC-TV's *Issues and Answers* that in regard to Europe "Washington is looking for action, not words."

In Europe, Undersecretary of Defense for Policy Robert W. Komer, the architect of the Rapid Deployment Force (or "Farce," as some military wags called it), met with the NATO Military Committee in Brussels to present a brutal set of demands. He requested the immediate acceleration of nuclear and conventional weapons "modernization," the build-up of military reserves, war materiel stockpilings, and greater NATO involvement in making its commercial airlines available for military airlifts into the Middle East. In short, the U.S. administration was demanding that Europe drop its commitment to détente and join Carter's *jihad* into the Middle East. The answer from Bonn and Paris was no.

Only days before the raid into Iran, Secretary of State Cyrus Vance tendered his resignation. "We haven't begun just an attack on Iran. We may have started World War III," said Vance to a friend. Together with a minority faction of the Carter administration and its Trilateral Commission supporters such as George Ball and Averell Harriman, Vance bailed out, convinced that Brzezinski was careening toward war.

Only hours after the failure of the raid had become known, and as the world recovered from its shock at the U.S. action and its incompetence, charges flew that the entire operation had been coordinated from beginning to end between Carter-Brzezinski and the Khomeini regime.

According to French intelligence sources, the final

details of the April 24 raid were the subject of a meeting held in Paris between Iran's Foreign Minister Ghotbzadeh and First Secretary Murphy of the U.S. embassy in France. The state-controlled Iraqi radio charged that the U.S. attack was "play-acting carried out in orchestration between Washington and Teheran." When White House Press Secretary Jody Powell was asked the day after the raid about prior collaboration between the Carter regime and Ghotbzadeh, he issued a stony "no comment."

The administration's explanation for the raid's failure—that it had been caused by the simultaneous failure of three of the eight helicopters used—was simply not believed. According to many reports, the real reason for the debacle of the U.S. action, in which a helicopter and a huge C-130 air transport plane reportedly collided on the ground in Iran and burst into flames while trying to flee, was Soviet military intervention. One source said that the raid failed when an overflight of Soviet Mig-21s staged a show of force directly above the American landing party, and the commander of the raiding force then decided to beat a hasty retreat, leading to a panic and the crash. Other sources with CIA connections reported that the U.S.S.R. had bombed the U.S. force almost as soon as it landed at the staging ground for Phase II of the raid, and that the administration's official version of the story was a coverup.

Is it possible that the raid may have been partly designed by Brzezinski and the National Security Council to test Soviet reaction to such a deployment? By sending a small force into Iran as occurred on April 24, Brzezinski may have been seeking to find out what Soviet units would be placed on alert, what missile sites and troop emplacements would be activated, what would be the posture of Soviet forces in Eastern Europe and along the China frontier, and so forth.

If this is the case, the U.S. raid into Iran was a dry run to test the U.S. strategic doctrine—first put forward by former Defense Secretary James Schlesinger—for a "limited nuclear war." Ever since the proclamation of the so-called Carter doctrine in January 1980, the United States had made it public that it intends to defend its "interests" in the Persian Gulf by force in case of a Soviet invasion from the north. But, every analyst knows, the Soviet Union has, by virtue of its proximity and its recent arms build-up program, an overwhelming conventional force advantage in the Middle East, so overwhelming, in fact, that if Moscow should decide to move into Iran or even the Arab Gulf states, the United States would have no adequate response—short of "tactical" nuclear warfare.

It is a given among experts that such a war could not be contained at the local level but would quickly escalate into all-out thermonuclear war. For this reason, many military authorities have found the Carter doctrine to be "insane."

Nevertheless, it was this doctrine that was officially proclaimed as American policy in Presidential Directive No. 59, issued in August 1980.

What is clear from the facts known about the April 24 raid is that the Carter administration, in going into Iran, had everything on its mind but an attempt to free the hostages. On the contrary, by charging into Iran with guns blazing, the U.S. administration guaranteed that the hostages would remain in Iran for months to come. It did this by strengthening the Khomeini forces, especially the extremists in the Islamic Republican Party led by Ayatollah Beheshti, at the expense of President Abolhassan Bani-Sadr.

In January 1980, the presidential election in Iran led to the victory of Bani-Sadr by an overwhelming margin of 75 percent. In ordinary times, the Parisian-trained Bani-Sadr would not be considered a moderate: he was a confirmed supporter of Khomeini, rigorously indoctrinated in the finer points of the lunatic fundamentalism now governing the country, and he was a fanatical advocate of imposing upon Iran the anti-industry genocidal policies of Cambodia's Pol Pot regime. Nevertheless, in the political spectrum of Iranian politics, Bani-Sadr was more amenable to a stable government than the mullahs of the IRP. He had gained the political support of what was left of Iran's urban intellectuals and middle class, many of whom privately despised him but viewed him as the lesser evil.

Secretary of State Cyrus Vance and British Foreign Secretary Lord Carrington had also hoped that Bani-Sadr might be able to pull together a government in Iran that could eventually ally itself to the U.S. NATO bloc on the basis of Muslim fundamentalism. To accomplish that, Vance and Carrington looked for a deal with Iran: release of the U.S. hostages in exchange for a resumed flow of arms and economic aid to Bani-Sadr's (and Khomeini's) Iran. In a press conference in February, President Carter declared that if the hostages were released, Washington would eagerly consider a "normal" relationship to Iran, including sending military aid to the regime.

The April 24 raid changed all that.

The failed U.S. action automatically precipitated a sudden rise in the strength of the extremists and ended whatever chance Bani-Sadr might have had to assemble a workable government. Occurring as it did only a few weeks before the Iranian parliamentary vote, it gave an enormous victory at the polls to the IRP and its mullahs, and handed Bani-Sadr's secular forces a resounding defeat. Because Khomeini had declared that it was the parliament that would assume the responsibility for deciding the fate of the U.S. hostages, that vote made it certain that the hostages would remain in Iran.

Until late December 1979, almost one year after the Khomeini revolution and more than seven weeks after the seizure of the American embassy, Captain Siavash Setoudeh, the defense attaché of the Iranian embassy in Washington, conducted his daily business inside the offices of the U.S. Office of Naval Research.

Setoudeh, representing a government with whom the United States was theoretically at the verge of war, worked under the direct supervision of the Office of Naval Intelligence and ONR, assisted by a sixteen-man team of Iranian terrorists and gun-runners. Within this highly sensitive facility at 800 North Quincy Street in Arlington, Virginia, accessible only to individuals with top security clearance, Captain Setoudeh, Captain Mansour, a recently arrived Iranian admiral, and a dozen other military agents of Ayatollah Khomeini's Islamic Republic of Iran worked with U.S. naval intelligence and with the approval of Zbigniew Brzezinski's National Security Council.

The Carter administration's alliance with the Khomeini regime had gone way beyond the negotiating stage.

At the end of December 1979, Setoudeh was expelled from his American offices, following widespread exposure of his presence and activities there by New Solidarity International Press Service and the *Executive Intelligence Review*. Despite Setoudeh's expulsion, the Pentagon and the State Department refused to make any comment on his activities or why he was allowed to use offices virtually inside the Pentagon itself.

Setoudeh was allowed to remain within the United States, returning to his original office in the Iranian embassy on Massachusetts Avenue—despite a presidential order one month earlier expelling all Iranian diplomats in retaliation for the seizure of the U.S. embassy.

Reportedly, the Iranian unit headed by Setoudeh was involved in coordinating the activities of Iranian students in at least forty American colleges and universities with which the Iranian military attaché had liaison. These activities included arms smuggling, gun running, and conduiting weapons to terrorist units sent from Iran into the United States.

In November 1979, just before the Setoudeh affair broke into the press, Ayatollah Khalkhali of the *Fedayeen-e Islam* (the Iranian branch of the Muslim Brotherhood) declared that he had sent killer squads into the United States to assassinate leading U.S. political figures and "enemies of the revolution," including a specified list of Iranians of the former regime.

According to Iranian sources, in the period after the takeover of the U.S. embassy in Teheran, at least 300 armed and well-trained Iranian terrorist personnel entered the United States on false passports with phony visas that were obtained from a visa stamp stolen from the occupied U.S. embassy. In an interview with the Paris-based *Libération* magazine, Khalkhali boasted that his teams have been trained "in the Middle East and in the United States itself."

The Setoudeh story broke in the following way.

On December 19, 1979, the New York offices of NSIPS news agency picked up rumors of direct collaboration between the Iranian embassy and the Pentagon. According to Iranian sources opposed to the Khomeini regime, Captain Setoudeh—who was described as a "naval liaison officer who is the defense attaché of the Iranian embassy"—could be found located at 800 North Quincy Street.

The next day, the NSIPS Washington bureau confirmed that the building in question was wholly owned and operated by the Office of Naval Research. An ONR spokesman, who refused to identify himself, said that the building was entirely occupied by offices containing U.S. military personnel, "except for a few foreigners who have reason for being there." He refused to elaborate.

That same day, an NSIPS investigative reporter called the offices of Captain Setoudeh, identifying herself as a representative of "a Hong Kong arms dealer." Setoudeh immediately came to the phone. When the caller said that her employer had instructed her to get in touch with Setoudeh to arrange a meeting for him "when he arrives in the country next week," the Iranian readily agreed.

Setoudeh was told that a "massive" arms shipment was coming into the United States "but outside normal channels." He replied: "That would be a good suggestion, to have a meeting together and discuss these things and then if we can do any help to this problem [sic], by all means. Otherwise, then we'll ship it to someone else in the country, or maybe in the embassy."

Setoudeh confirmed, twice, that he is the "proper person" to handle such matters. He asked only, "Could you tell me only which force is your company dealing with? Is it the air force? The navy? Which one?" He also said that he would be glad to clear his entire schedule for the next week—"even Christmas Day"—to meet the "arms dealer."

Queried about his status in the United States because of President Carter's expulsion order issued on December 12, Setoudeh laughed and replied, "That doesn't apply to me." (In fact, at this time, more than two weeks after the order was given, not a single one of the 183 Iranian diplomats ordered to leave had gone, and Iran's embassy and consulates were functioning normally. Not one official did leave, until Washington broke relations with Iran four months later.)

At the Iranian embassy, a spokesman for Chargé d'Affaires Ali Agha confirmed that Setoudeh was the embassy's military attaché.

That afternoon, two reporters from NSIPS paid an unannounced visit to Captain Setoudeh's office to see what they might discover. At the entrance to the imposing building, the only identification sign read: "Office of Naval Research." Inside, a sleepy, Christmas-minded guard waved the reporters on.

Upstairs, they found a bustling office filled with Iranians. The walls were covered with portraits of Ayatollah Khomeini, revolutionary slogans, and other signs and symbols confirming that the office was indeed loyal to the Khomeini regime.

When the reporters began questioning several of those present and taking photographs of the office and its decor, pandemonium broke loose. "You can't do that!" shouted an Iranian officer, who later identified himself as Captain Mansour. Amid the ensuing chaos, the office did admit that it was occupying U.S. government space. For a period of fifteen minutes, the two Americans were physically detained by Khomeini's military representatives; they were threatened and their film confiscated by force.

Immediately afterward, the NSIPS correspondents went to the press briefing by Jody Powell, the spokesman for President Carter, at the White House. The NSIPS reporter put before the press and Mr. Powell the preliminary results of the investigation. But Powell—like the State Department earlier—had no explanation for the presence of Setoudeh in the secret offices of Naval Research. Nor would the White House or the State Department comment on why the Iranian diplomats had not left the country in the face of the order from the President that they be ousted.

At the State Department briefing, Hodding Carter III was equally uncommunicative, promising to answer the questions after checking with Secretary of State Vance. After the briefing, however, State's Near East Affairs public information chief George Sherman told one of the NSIPS correspondents that "I might be able to help you a little more if you will tell me why you are asking that question."

A dozen offices of the Pentagon all refused comment.

By the following day, December 21, reporters in Washington, including the White House correspondents for several major national networks and leading Washington dailies, were now looking into the story. That same day NSIPS called Captain Setoudeh for a telephone interview. He was asked his function.

"This is the office dealing with students in American universities," he said, after some hesitation. "I deal with both military students and civilians, especially those in engineering courses." According to Setoudeh, at each university in the country where Iranian students are present—and he claimed over forty—"there is a military liaison officer."

Setoudeh's admission that he coordinates student activities touched off another important line of investigation. Quickly, NSIPS established that Setoudeh was a close collaborator of Abolfazl Nahidian; he has admitted meeting with Nahidian on several occasions. Nahidian, who purports to be a Washington rug merchant with offices on Wisconsin Avenue, is a top coordinator of Savama, Khomeini's secret police, in the United States. In his business, Nahidian travels back and forth between Washington and Teheran, and he is an outspoken supporter of Ayatollah Khomeini.

Reportedly, aside from rugs, Nahidian has been involved in conduiting millions of dollars since the Iranian revolution to pro-Khomeini terrorist groups in the United States. Many of the 300 Iranian students who reportedly came through U.S. ports of entry bearing phony visas were shuttled into the Nahidian-Setoudeh circles and then into safehouses around the country. One of Nahidian's bodyguards, David Belfield (a.k.a. Daoud Salahuddin), is alleged to have been the murderer of Ali Tabatabai, an anti-Khomeini Iranian who headed the Iran Freedom Foundation, assassinated in Maryland on July 22, 1980.

No law enforcement personnel came to congratulate

NSIPS on its exposure of Nahidian and Setoudeh. Top administration officials were tight-lipped and refused all comment. A few days after the story broke, Setoudeh was quietly moved to the Iranian embassy. Reporters attempting to find out why Setoudeh was allowed into those premises and what his connection to the Pentagon was were politely but firmly rebuffed, and no more was heard of Captain Setoudeh.

Given the Carter administration's alliance with the Khomeini regime on every level, the question emerges: Who controls the "students" who hold the hostages? Who are they?

When the U.S. embassy was taken over, a previously unknown organization calling itself "Students Following the Iman's Line" was identified as the group that led the seizure. (The "Imam," of course, is Khomeini.) the leader of the organization was said to be a dentist named Dr. Habibollah Peyman, who worked closely with Ayatollah Khoini, an obscure mullah.

The students' organization is officially part of Ayatollah Khalkhali's *Fedayeen-e Islam*, and works with the so-called Party of God (*Hizbollahi*) militia. The Hizbollahi is feared in Iran because of its gangster tactics and frequent use of violence, acting as a strike force—or a kind of SS—on behalf of the radical faction of the Islamic Republican Party.

According to Iranian intelligence sources, the students' leader, Dr. Peyman, spent many years outside of Iran, during the era of the Shah, primarily in Europe. During this time, Peyman was a paid agent of the Mossad, Israel's foreign intelligence service.

The relationship exposes one of the secrets of the

Ayatollah Khomeini. The Mossad runs like a thread throughout the command structure of the Islamic fundamentalist regime. For example, while involved with the plasma physics program at Berkeley, in California, Mustafa Chamran, Khomeini's defense minister, made connection with an extremist faction of the Mossad via circles associated with Professor Yuval Neeman. Neeman, an advanced theoretical physicist, is the father of Israel's nuclear weapons capability and the founder of the ultra-nationalist Tekhiya Party in Israel. For a time, Neeman was a visiting professor at the University of Texas at Austin, where he reputedly also established ties to Ibrahim Yazdi, then at Baylor University in Texas.

After he left Berkeley, Chamran went to Lebanon where he became the commander of a violent Shiite extremist group called Al Amal, which maintained ties to both Colonel Muammar Qaddafi in Libya and to Shiite radicals in Lebanon, Syria, and Iran. In Lebanon, Chamran worked with radical factions of the Palestinian guerrilla movement, especially those believed to be presently under the control of Israeli intelligence. (The Israelis often use terror by "Palestinian extremists" to bolster Israel's position both internally and in the West.) When the Iranian revolution started, Chamran went to Iraq to see Khomeini and traveled with him to Paris. Since then, the Al Amal organization has become overtly pro-Israeli and anti-PLO.

In the aftermath of Khomeini's takeover, Chamran and Yazdi took control of the enormous apparatus of Savak, working closely with General Fardoust. Today, Israel's Mossad is believed to have a disproportionate influence in the inner councils of the Khomeini regime. The extent of its influence is not known, but the fact that the Mossad-tainted Chamran and Yazdi gained control of the Savak organization has given them enormous power.

So far, we have found that the "Islamic fundamentalist revolution" that seized power in February 1979 was instigated by British Petroleum, was given crucial assistance by a NATO general, forged a continuing alliance with the "Satan" government of the United States, and is heavily penetrated by the Israeli secret intelligence service. Now we answer the question: who is the Ayatollah Khomeini?

4

Savak's
Insane Ayatollah

It is August 1953. The rollercoaster reign of Prime Minister Mohammed Mossadegh is coming to an end. After several years as the leader of Iran's almost successful republican revolution, the tide is beginning to turn, and the U.S. Central Intelligence Agency is preparing to bring the Shah back to Iran and restore him to the throne. Several years before, Mossadegh had ridden to power with the support of Iran's communists and, especially, with the power provided him by several leaders of the Shiite clergy. Now, in 1953, the clergy has abandoned Mossadegh. Their unofficial leader is Ayatollah Kashani, a mullah cast more in the tradition of an Al Capone gangster than a religious leader. Together with another mullah named Shams Qanad-Abadi, Ayatollah Kashani commands an empire of street gangs and religious fanatics. Now the CIA is ready to use them.

In Teheran, agent Kermit "Kim" Roosevelt is passing out funds to the city's underworld for a made-to-order "demonstration" in support of the Shah. The several thousands of demonstrators, who are even now trying to memorize the slogans they will chant, are only window-dressing for the operation that, in a matter of hours, will turn the tables on the prime minister.

It is at least marginally useful politically, the CIA reasons, to have some chanting Loyalists in the streets clamoring for the Shah, if only for newsreel footage and the world press. But the real "revolution" against Mossadegh is a decision that has already been taken by the leaders of the American, British, and Israeli secret services and the boards of major international oil companies. It is their petty cash that finances the mob demonstrations, and it is Ayatollah Kashani who "gets out the troops."

Lost among the 5,000 or so demonstrators shouting "Long Live the Shah!" is an obscure mullah named Ruhollah Khomeini.

It is one of the finer ironies of history that the man responsible for bringing down the Shah in 1979 was a paid agent of the monarchist forces twenty-five years earlier. The complete story of Khomeini's life probably will not be known for some time, but enough is known already about the mullah who has brought the Middle Ages back to Iran to enable us to judge what kind of a man he is today.

To begin with, his name is not really Khomeini; he selected the name "Ruhollah Khomeini" for himself sometime in the 1930s. Because his grandfather was born in Kashmir, India and the family was originally of Indian Muslim origin, one of Khomeini's brothers chose the

name "Hindi," reportedly because of his business dealings with India. Some reports say that Khomeini himself
was not even born in Iran, but in India, and migrated to
Iran in his early youth.

Some sixty years ago, during the upheavals in Iran in
the early 1920s, when the late Shah's father Reza Khan
Pahlavi was in the process of seizing power, young
Khomeini received his first political battle-scars. At the
time, the young Reza Pahlavi conferred with the leader
of the republican revolution in Turkey, the famous
Ataturk. Ataturk urged the brash young military officer
to follow his example and to establish a constitutional
republic in Persia, urging Pahlavi to reject the concept
of a monarchy as too rigid and confining, inappropriate
for a modernizing nation. Initially, Reza considered the
idea—until violent uprisings of the Iranian clergy forced
him to decide in favor of a monarchy. And so he became
Reza Shah. Khomeini, then in his teens and reportedly
bearing a grudge against Reza for having somehow been
involved in the death of his father, joined the mullahs'
protest.

Decades later, it was the same Khomeini who would
be the bitterest foe of the monarch—but not before he
and his brother had become part of Ayatollah Kashani's
drive to put Reza's son on the throne.

The CIA was not the only agency sponsoring the
1953 overthrow of Mossadegh. Ayatollah Kashani was
close to the leaders of the Muslim Brotherhood in Iran,
the *Fedayeen-e Islam*. In the 1950s, the acknowledged
leader of the Fedayeen was Ayatollah Navabsafavi. With
between 200 and 300 members, the Fedayeen had been
in secret existence since the early 1940s, when the
Brotherhood's apparatus in Egypt—which itself had

been cut out of whole cloth by the British intelligence service—extended its reach into Iran. The Iranian branch of the Brotherhood was known almost exclusively for its spectacular assassinations, including the murders of at least two prime ministers.

British secret intelligence's influence over Iran's clergymen was no secret, even many years ago. "Many influential clergymen formed alliances with representatives of foreign powers, most often the British," wrote the Shah's twin sister, Ashraf Pahlavi, in her book *Faces In A Mirror*. "And there was, in fact, a standing joke in Persia that said if you picked up a clergyman's beard, you would see the words 'Made in England' stamped on the other side." After World War II, says Ashraf, "With the encouragement of the British, who saw the mullahs as an effective counterforce to the Communists, the elements of the extreme religious right were starting to surface again, after years of being suppressed."

Kashani and the "religious right" based their power on the shocktroops of organized crime in Iran. In Iran, the mafia is called *chaqou-kesh*. The words mean "knife slayers" in Persian, derived from their trademark of stabbing people to death with concealed daggers.

The Iranian mafia is found in the bazaars, the marketplaces, especially in the critical fruit and vegetable markets.° From this powerful base, it also controls prostitution, gambling—and especially the extremely lucrative narcotics racket. Like some exotic version of a New York or Chicago "godfather," in 1953 Ayatollah

---

° In 1978, a CIA official told me that the mafia controls nearly all food production and distribution in Iran.

Kashani simply ordered his lieutenants to put together a rent-a-mob for the CIA.

After the 1953 putsch, with the Shah back in power, a certain military officer named Teymour Bakhtiar emerged into the limelight. Promoted to the position of general and then named military governor of Teheran and director of army intelligence, Bakhtiar became a trusted aide to the Shah. In 1957, when the State Security and Intelligence Organization (Savak) was establshed, Bakhtiar became its first director. From the start, Iran's new intelligence service received a great deal of support from Israel's Mossad, especially relying on Israeli torture specialists.

The Savak also began to put on its payroll a vast army of mullahs and ayatollahs, preferring those with links to the *chaqou-kesh.* Salaries from Savak to the mullahs ranged from as low as $100 a month to as high as $1,000 a month. One of the people placed on the Savak payroll was Ruhollah Khomeini—at a stipend of $300 per month.

At the time, Khomeini was a low-ranking teacher at the important theological center of Qom, Iran. Reports in the *New York Times* and elsewhere have tried to portray Khomeini's role in Qom as a major scholar of religious law and an advocate of the system of Plato's *Republic.* It is there, that Khomeini, acting as a parody of the fanatical mullah, began to build his cult following.

The Israeli connection to Savak at this time undoubtedly penetrated deep into Iran's Islamic fundamentalist clergy; it would not be surprising to find that agents of the Israeli intelligence service made contact with Khomeini as early as 1957. In that year, there were eleven Mossad and Shin Beth agents in Iran to help organize

Savak. By 1976 over 500 Israeli intelligence personnel were stationed in Teheran, where they were involved in almost every branch of the Savak apparatus. The Mossad's influence was reputed to be concentrated in the supersecret Special Intelligence Bureau, established as an independent entity inside the Savak. The Bureau's chief was General Hossein Fardoust. Through Savak and the Special Intelligence Bureau, the entire organization of mullahs was penetrated and controlled. "There were only two kinds of mullahs in Iran in the 1950s," said an informed source. "Those that were pro-Savak, and those that were in jail." Khomeini was not in jail.

Teymour Bakhtiar was a sadist, who developed a reputation for the cruelest sorts of tortures and confinement. But he was also an agent of the British—and the Kennedy administration.

After John F. Kennedy came to the White House in 1961, Washington soon began placing enormous pressures on the Shah of Iran. The Shah had been showing unfortunate signs of wanting to cooperate with the non-Seven Sisters oil companies, especially Italy's state-sector oil company, ENI. To reassert control over Iran's oil for the Anglo-American consortium, headed by British Petroleum, Kennedy threatened the Shah's regime.° In January 1961, coinciding almost to the day with Kennedy's inauguration, demonstrations and protests in Iran, mostly sponsored by communists and the clergy, exploded the country. Early in 1961, Kennedy sent Averell Harriman, the former New York governor and patrician, to present the U.S. demands to the Shah. Behind the

---

° At about the same time, ENI's chairman Enrico Mattei was assassinated.

scenes, Bakhtiar was secretly funding anti-Shah demonstrators with Savak funds. The Shah realized that Bakhtiar was acting as a traitor, and he dismissed him from his position as head of the Savak. Several other top-ranking military men were fired at the same time. But a few months later, under pressure of a teachers' strike that led to violence, the Shah bowed to the pressure from Kennedy and Harriman and installed Ali Amini as the new prime minister. It was rumored that Teymour Bakhtiar had been working to stir up the teachers' demonstrations.

The organizer of the teachers' strike was Mohammed Derakhshesh, an opportunist who hired himself out as a spy for the British and who became minister of education in the Amini Cabinet; eighteen years later, Derakhshesh would travel to the United States to meet the National Security Council through Richard Cottam, the University of Pittsburgh professor and former CIA agent. The Shah himself confirmed, in an interview several years ago in *Newsweek*, that Kennedy forced him to name Amini as prime minister. When, asked about such reports, the Shah declared: "It's past history but correct."

In 1962, the Shah visited Washington for a face-to-face meeting with Kennedy. Earlier that year, the Shah had also confronted Bakhtiar with the evidence of his sedition and fomenting of rebellion, whereupon Bakhtiar fled Iran into exile in Switzerland. Now, in his meeting with Kennedy, the Shah proposed an amicable agreement: if Kennedy would allow the Shah to oust Prime Minister Amini, he would agree to the policies demanded by Washington. Upon his return to Iran, the Shah fired Amini—and then reneged on the deal. Kennedy was enraged.

Thus, later that year the American president called General Bakhtiar to the United States.

Ostensibly arriving in the country for medical treatment, Bakhtiar flew in from Switzerland and went directly to the White House, where he met with JFK. The subject of the meeting: to plot against the Shah. The means they selected: Ruhollah Khomeini.

During the previous year, the elderly ayatollah had been working extensively with General Bakhtiar's Savak. Building a reputation for himself as an uncompromising, fanatical ideologue, Khomeini was fast becoming for more and more Iranians a cult hero. It was Khomeini who would be pushed forward to lead the fight against the Shah's 1963 "White Revolution."

The White Revolution was the Shah's project to undercut the power of the reactionary opposition, which for many years had been a British asset.

"Who were the British agents in Teheran who led the anti-Shah revolts of 1963?" A broadcast of the *Free Voice of Iran*, an anti-Khomeini radio station, on June 5, 1980, explained: "The British mercenaries in Iran could generally be classified into four groups. The first group was the paid politicians and journalists . . . whose numerous treacheries were revealed during the struggle for the nationalization of the oil industry, after which they were greatly weakened and did not have the power to stand up. The second was the Freemasons, the treacherous members of which were and continue to be the tools of British policy and protectors of British interests in Iran.

"The third group of agents implementing British policies in Iran were some of the *khans*, feudalists, and big landowners whose filthy face in treason against the

homeland and service to the British Empire has been
revealed on many occasions in the course of Iran's
history. . . . Finally, some of [the] pseudoclergy have
been on Britain's payroll for a long time."

It was the alliance between the Freemasons, the old
landowners, and the clergy that mounted the operation
against the Shah in 1963. Its leader was Khomeini, but
only as a symbol.

Concerning Khomeini, the *Free Voice of Iran* reports
that "since the days he was a religious student, he
received rations from the British, and under the label of
'monthly tuition' from the proceeds of the Indian *awqaf*
[religious affairs department], received monthly payments from British agents and was in constant contact
with his masters."

In 1962, the bearded ayatollah with the evil stare
issued his first major proclamation, attacking the government's plan to enfranchise women as a violation of the
status of women under Islam. Then, in 1963, when the
White Revolution was underway, Khomeini had his first
serious confrontation with the Shah—ten years after he
had marched in the streets to bring the monarch to
power.

The White Revolution challenged Iran's old families,
since it expropriated feudal estates and either handed
them over to peasants or turned them into state cooper-
atives. The act struck at the heart of the feudal-clergy
alliance. By January 1963, Khomeini was arrested for
issuing angry pamphlets accusing the Shah of violating
Islam's precepts by the nationalization measures. Islam
guarantees the sanctity of private property, Khomeini
argued.

Though Khomeini was acting clearly on behalf of the
landlords and the British, his cult followers took to the

streets. Clumsy arrests of Khomeini partisans by the police and the Savak—which may have been seeking a provocation and probably was working in collaboration with Khomeini and Bakhtiar—fueled the protests even more. During the religious holidays of that year, Khomeini's movement grew into an all-out rebellion. Portraits of Khomeini stared down from the bazaars and the mosques. In early June 1963, he was arrested by the police for the first time, then released two months later after an "understanding" was reached. He was arrested twice again, in October 1963 and in May 1964. In October 1964 he was finally sent into exile by the Shah.

Meanwhile, General Bakhtiar had quietly moved from his Swiss headquarters to Iraq, where he operated secretly in Baghdad. British influence in Iraq was then particularly strong, and General Bakhtiar cooperated closely with the British embassy in Teheran to fuel the anti-Shah riots and support the Khomeini movement. Over 5,000 people were killed in two years of violent demonstrations.

The Shah minced no words concerning his opposition: "We are done with social and political parasites," he said. "I abhor black reaction even more than red destruction."

Hinting at the connections of the rebels to Britain, the Shah declared, "The agents of foreign influence in Iran were the politicians, the feudal lords . . . some self-styled religious leaders who ever since the establishment of the constitutional monarchy were generally known to be at the beck and call of one foreign power in particular."

When he was exiled, Khomeini's choice of refuges revealed whose "black reaction" it was. He fled first to Izmir, Turkey, site of the NATO installation, where he stayed for a period; he then traveled to Baghdad, Iraq, where he contacted the networks around General Bakhtiar.

Together, Khomeini, Bakhtiar, and British intelligence continued to stir up trouble in Iran. During the rest of the 1960s Bakhtiar was involved in several conspiracies, including the 1965 assassination of Prime Minister Ali Mansour and a botched assassination attempt against the Shah.

Traveling between Geneva, Paris, Rome, Beirut, and Baghdad, Bakhtiar built up his connections throughout the Mediterranean world. One of his closest associates was François Porteau de la Morandière, a member of the extremist Secret Army Organization that was responsible for the repeated assassination attempts against French President Charles de Gaulle. Bakhtiar also strengthened his links to the underworld, procuring his funds through drug smuggling and gun running.

In 1970, in August, he was killed in what was said to be a hunting accident in the hills of Iraq near the Iranian border. There is little question that he was assassinated on orders from the Shah. Later that year, Iran announced the discovery of a plot to overthrow the government led by partisans of General Bakhtiar, and hundreds of military men were arrested.

For Khomeini, now a lonely mullah in Iraq, his chief sponsor and patron was dead.

Khomeini's return to Iran on February 1, 1979, marked the end of a years' long British campaign to destabilize Iran. Not for a moment during his exile was Khomeini out of the control of the British intelligence service.

With the coming to power in 1968 of the Iraqi government of the Arab Baath Socialist Party, Khomeini was kept under a careful watch by the Iraqi authorities, who did not want him stirring up trouble among the very large Shiite community of Iraq. In the mid-1970s, he was found lending his support to the rebellion of Iraq's Kurdish tribes in the north. But because of his status as a religious leader, the Iraqis believed it impossible to arrest him.

Today Khomeini is a character out of a Kipling novel. According to those who have known him, he is a vegetable, and is said to sleep up to twenty-two hours a day, awaking only for a dazed excursion into the real world for a few hours. He is rarely rational. His son Ahmad Khomeini told *Le Figaro* magazine that his father is usually "in another world" and that he "doesn't pay attention anymore to what is happening around him."

Khomeini resembles nothing so much as the fictional Wizard of Oz, a puffed-up puppet whose controls are operated from behind the scenes. For the most part, his declarations and pompous pronouncements are statements issued in his name, or statements written for him by his intimate circle of advisers.

But Iranian politics today is dependent on the symbol of Khomeini and on his authority as the "imam," and Iran's battling political factions must win the approval of the drooling ayatollah for any major decision. No sooner has one faction of Khomeini's advisers spent time coaxing the senile fool into adopting some position concerning an issue of importance than they leave and in comes another coterie, prepared to persuade His Eminence of the opposite point of view. By manipulating the aged man, Iran's factions wield life or death power over their rivals. Reasoned argument, of course, does not work with Khomeini; more useful is an argument that is based on accusing one's opponents of anti-Islamic behavior or "warring against God."

Hence, political decisions in Iran over the period since the revolution are always subject to instant reversal. President Bani-Sadr has several times lined up the imam's support for some policy or initiative, only to find a day or two later that Khomeini has reversed position and sided with the more extreme, fundamentalist faction around Ayatollah Khalkhali.

There is another reason for this. Many people believe that the depraved Khalkhali is, in effect, Khomeini's boss, since Khalkhali is the head of the feared *Fedayeen-e Islam*. According to French sources, Khomeini himself is a member of the Fedayeen and is therefore subject to organizational discipline under Khalkhali.

The Ayatollah Sadegh Khalkhali is a mystery man in Iran. He holds no official position in the government, but he wields enormous power. In the first months after the revolution, it was Khalkhali who served as the unofficial judge and executioner for hundreds, probably thousands, of political prisoners. His sadistic temperament and lust for blood earned him the nickname "Judge Blood." He is a certified lunatic, and spent a number of years in a mental asylum for torturing and killing small animals, such as cats and birds. Wags have called him Ayatollah Khatkhiller.

More recently, Khalkhali has served as the head of Iran's antidrug program, a sick joke given the fact the Fedayeen is probably the biggest drug-smuggling ring in Iran. From this position, he has used his authority to order hundreds more executions of people condemned to death allegedly as drug traffickers—but, in fact, guilty only of political opposition to Khomeini's rule.

Following the raid into Iran by U.S. forces last April 24, Khalkhali gained notoriety for displaying the dead bodies of American servicemen killed in the action, including holding up charred pieces of flesh and bone.

Now, he is said to live inside the depths of Qasr Prison outside Teheran, location for most of the secret trials and brutal, machine-gun executions of Khomeini's enemies. Like a sewer rat, he scuttles through the dungeons, gleefully clapping his hands at this or that little irony of his task. Once, during a macabre guided tour of the prison for reporters, Khalkhali delivered his lecture in between eating mouthfuls of vanilla ice cream from a gallon tub that he carried with him. At the end of the tour, when several reporters' questions angered him, he threatened to have them all executed right then and there. The reporters hastily departed.

For many, it may be hard to understand how a nation could allow itself to be ruled by such madmen. Khomeini and Khalkhali are truly insane. But the conditions of their rule must be understood.

Millions of Iranians, especially those of the middle class, have fled the country rather than endure the regime's horrors; according to U.S. government estimates, up to six million people may have left Iran since 1978. Those that remain live under the gun of the Revolutionary Guard and the *komitehs*, or Revolutionary Committees.

At the beginning, because many Iranians chafed under the Shah's one-man rule, they naively thought that by supporting Khomeini's movement they could rid themselves of the monarchy, and then dispense with Khomeini. Such was not to be the case. With the passing of time, most of Khomeini's support has dissipated, leaving only the cult followers of the Muslim Brotherhood. It is that section of Iran's population upon which Khomeini's rule now rests exclusively, and the insane mind of the mullah is perfectly matched to its constituency.

In any developing country, the ruler—if he is even remotely concerned with his country's welfare—is faced with the fundamental problem: how to end the misery and backwardness of the rural peasants and their donkeylike life. The peasant existence has been entrenched in that mode of day-to-day life for many centuries, and the mind of the peasant—uneducated and unaware of the world outside—is locked at a level not much higher than his beasts of burden. Such a population is desperately in need of an education program, to enable it to become capable of assimilating modern technology. Without that, without the beginnings of progress making itself felt on the mind of the peasant, he is condemned to a hell more horrible than anything described in Dante's *Inferno*.

The life of rural idiocy makes the peasant population vulnerable to manipulation or bribery that molds it into a "popular rebellion." So with Khomeini: his chief supporters were not the skilled workers of Iran, nor the middle class, but the millions of displaced peasants with little education who had streamed into Iran's cities and eked out an existence in the shantytowns and the slums of southern Teheran.

In the Middle East, for fifty centuries such populations have been reduced to dependency on the priesthood, going back to the days when the cults of the ancient world dominated political life. Often described as "magicians" or sorcerers, cult priests have used the tricks of psychology and superstition to weave a mystical web of enchantment around their followers. Their techniques include the use of psychosexual fears, fantasies, and drugs. So with Khomeini. If one could truly enter into the mind of a mullah like Khomeini or Khalkhali, perhaps then one would fully comprehend the pure evil that is represented there.

Recently, translated into English, there has appeared a book in which Khomeini's proclamations have been gathered into one place from several of his works. The book's maxims appear incredible and even laughable to us, but one must consider them from the vantage point of their intended audience. For these pathetic people, troubled not by concerns of politics, business, law, or even more simple problems such as which television program to watch, Khomeini's word is law. Their concerns arise out of an unfathomable depth of backwardness verging on the insane, rooted in superstition.

"There are eleven things which are impure," Khomeini declares. "Urine, excrement, sperm, bones, blood, dogs, pigs, non-Muslim men and women, wine, beer, and the sweat of the excrement-eating camel." He adds, "Wine and all other intoxicating beverages are impure, but opium and hashish are not."

Says Khomeini; "It is forbidden to consume the excrement of animals or their nasal secretions. But if such are mixed in minute proportions into other foods their consumption is not forbidden. The meat of horses, mules, or donkeys is not recommended. It is strictly forbidden if the animal was sodomized while alive by a man. In that case, the animal must be taken outside the city and sold.

"If one commits an act of sodomy with a cow, a ewe, or a camel, their urine and their excrements become impure, and even their milk may no longer be consumed. The animal must quickly be killed and the price of it paid to its owner by him who sodomized it," says Khomeini.

Khomeini himself is reported by many sources to be a practicing homosexual, which is not uncommon—is even the rule—among the mullahs. During his years in exile, especially in Paris, his sexual partner was said to be Sadegh Ghotbzadeh, Iran's foreign minister. Ghotbzadeh reportedly is a notorious homosexual-sadist, like Khalkhali, and the fact that he is not married has long been the subject of jokes among Iranians. Given this background, Khomeini prescribes in great detail on the sexual habits of his followers:

"During the time a woman is menstruating, it is preferable for a man to avoid coitus, even if it does not involve full penetration—that is, as far as the circumcision ring—and even if it does not involve ejaculation. It is also highly inadvisable for him to sodomize her during this time."

Other superstitions are covered by Khomeini:

"*Namaze-ayat* is the name given to the prayer to be said when one witnesses natural phenomena that inspire fear. This prayer is required in the four following cases: total or partial eclipse of the sun; total or partial eclipse of the moon; earthquake, even though it not be fearsome; and thunder, lightning, and black or red winds. If several of these phenomena occur simultaneously, for instance, if an eclipse should be accompanied by an earthquake, two prayers are required. In case of earthquake or lightning or thunder, one must pray immediately; failing to do so is a sin which is not pardoned until after this prayer is said, no matter how much later, even to the last day of a person's life."

Endless rules and regulations are put forward by the ayatollah concerning when and how to pray, to eat, to drink, to go to the bathroom. "When defecating or urinating, one must squat in such a way as neither to face Mecca nor to turn one's back upon it," he says. On prayer: "If a person who is praying turns red in the face from suppressing an impulse to burst out laughing, that person must start the prayer over again. . . . Clapping one's hands or jumping up in the air during a prayer makes it null and void." And so forth.

Khomeini's insane version of Islam has made him the subject of ridicule among other Muslims, both Sunni and Shia. Many of the highest authorities in the Muslim world, among the *ulema* (clergy) in particular, condemn him as a heretic for, among other reasons—probably the most sacrilegious thing that a Muslim could say—claiming that he himself is more powerful than the Prophet Mohammed. Many Shia resent the fact that Khomeini has usurped the title of the "imam," for that title is an extremely solemn one for those of the Shiite faith. Many even argue that Khomeini cannot even legitimately be called an "ayatollah."

How long will the world continue to be plagued with the mad ayatollah? Of course, he is very old, and he has had several heart attacks. Many Iranians expect him to die quite soon, and there are a number of political power centers that would like him dead immediately—even if not by strictly natural causes. One thing is certain: when Khomeini dies, there is no one that can replace him. He is the unique focus of his cult following in Iran. When he dies he leaves a profound vacuum of power.

The most likely result will be the eruption of a civil war in Iran, in which the two most powerful forces will be the Communists, especially strong in the north of Iran, and the conservative opposition to Khomeini, including the military and some of the tribes such as the Kurds; joining the latter will probably be many of the more moderate religious leaders who presently are held hostage to Khomeini's lunacy, such as Ayatollah Shareatmadari.

For thousands of Iranians, whatever the outcome, Khomeini's death cannot come too soon.

5

Muslim Brotherhood I: Britain's Plot Against Islam

"We have nothing against going to the moon, or setting up atomic installations," says Khomeini in his *Green Book*. "But we too have a mission to accomplish: the mission of serving Islam and making its sacred principles known to the entire world, in the hope that all the monarchs and presidents of republics throughout the Muslim world will finally recognize that our cause is just, and by that very fact become submissive to us. Naturally, we have no desire to strip them of their functions; we will allow them to retain power, provided they show themselves to be obedient and worthy of our confidence."

Who is this "we" that Khomeini says the heads of state of all Muslim nations must become subservient to? The ayatollah has let slip where his true allegiance lies— not to Islam, but to the secret society known as the

Muslim Brotherhood—the "we" who "have a mission to accomplish."

The Muslim Brotherhood is a London creation, forged as the standard-bearer of an ancient, antireligious (pagan) heresy that has plagued Islam since the establishment of the Islamic community *(umma)* by the Prophet Mohammed in the seventh century. Representing organized Islamic fundamentalism, the organization called the Muslim Brotherhood (*Ikhwan al-Muslimun* in Arabic) was officially founded in Egypt, in 1929, by the British agent Hasan al-Banna, a Sufi mystic. Today, the Muslim Brotherhood is the umbrella under which a host of fundamentalist Sufi, Sunni, and radical Shiite brotherhoods and societies flourish.

The real story of the Muslim Brotherhood is more fantastic than the mere imagination of the authors of espionage novels could create. It functions as a conspiracy; its members exchange coded greetings and secret passwords; although no formal membership list exists, its members are organized into hierarchical cells or "lodges" like the European freemason societies and orders. The Muslim Brotherhood does not respect national frontiers; it spans the entire Islamic world. Some of its members are government officials, diplomats, and military men; others are street gangsters and fanatics. While the leaders of the Muslim Brotherhood are at home in plush-carpeted paneled board rooms of top financial institutions, at the lower levels the Muslim Brotherhood is a paramilitary army of thugs and assassins.

At its highest level, the Muslim Brotherhood is not Muslim. Nor is it Christian, Jewish, or part of any religion. In the innermost council are men who change their religion as easily as other men might change their shirts.

Taken together, the generic Muslim Brotherhood does not belong to Islam, but to the pre-Islamic barbarian cults of mother-goddess worship that prevailed in ancient Arabia. As much as the peddlers of mythology might want us to believe that the Muslim Brotherhood and Ayatollah Khomeini represent a legitimate expression of a deeply rooted "sociological phenomenon," it is not the case. Nor does the Muslim Brotherhood represent more than a tiny fraction of the world's Muslim believers.

The Muslim Brotherhood could not exist today were it not for the fact that the more backward elements of Muslim culture were observed, taken note of, and then carefully cultivated by Orientalists of the British Oxford and Cambridge universities. The *Ikhwan* is the result of the patient organizing by London's agents in the Islamic world, men such as the famous T. E. Lawrence ("of Arabia"), Wilfrid Scawen Blunt, E. G. Browne, Harry St.-J. B. Philby, Arnold Toynbee, and Bertrand Russell.

For Americans, British sponsorship of the Muslim Brotherhood should not be surprising. The policy of the British Empire was to maintain London's colonies in a state of underdevelopment. In the Middle East, the British have always sought out the corrupt tribal leaders and the venal clergy to lead movements whose objectives have always seemed to coincide with British objectives. With the Muslim Brotherhood, British imperial policy was institutionalized in the form of a disciplined organization dedicated to returning the Middle East to the Dark Ages.

The cultivation of backwardness by an established

oligarchy is nothing new. Within Islamic history, the great proponents of antiscientific doctrines, mysticism, and nominalism—such as the ninth-century Al-Ashari and the eleventh-century Al-Ghazali—were paid agents for the aristocrats of the caliphate and later kingdoms, who sought to disorganize the emerging rationalist tendency and its later magnificent expression in the work of the humanist geniuses Al-Farabi, Ibn Sina, and Hasan ibn al-Sabbah. The irrationalist tendency within Islam was revived, in the nineteenth century and afterward, by the British. It was the British who sponsored the higher education system in the Muslim world; the British who funded the publication of Islam's obscurantists; and the British who held learned conferences to proclaim the worth of a specifically "non-Western" brand of "Muslim science." The British goal was to convince the Muslim world that its "true" culture was backwardness and irrationality. Important in this process was a century-long British project to explain the decline of Islam: according to the London view, the collapse of the great Muslim empires and their eventual domination by the imperialist powers was the result of an inherent weakness, or defect, within the "Muslim psyche."

In this chapter, we will uncover the roots of the Muslim Brotherhood. We will take a look at its precedent organizations in the Middle Ages, and we will see how the British Orientalists used their knowledge of these early movements and cults to eventually found the organization that stands behind the Ayatollah Khomeini.

The Islamic revolution of the early seventh century was the accomplishment of a single man, the Prophet Mohammed, one of the greatest political and religious leaders in history. In a few short decades, Mohammed singlehandedly established in Arabia an empire that within eighty years stretched from southern France and Spain through North Africa and Asia to the borders of China.

The enemy of early Christianity had been the pagan cults of the Roman Empire, who, failing to destroy the religion from without, attempted to pervert it from within. The enemy of Mohammed's Islam was the pre-Islamic mother cults that remained, in disguise, buried within the Muslim environment, supplying the roots for what would become the Muslim Brotherhood.

The key to Mohammed's achievement was his ability to establish his authority as a teacher to the worldly merchants of Arabia and to the nomadic Bedouin tribesmen alike. Pagan, pre-Islamic Arabia existed in a state of near psychosis. The Bedouins, and even the settled Arabs and traders, lived in a terrifying world of demons and *jinn* ("genies"), representing the fearful, personified natural phenomena that dominated the desert. Gnomes and "earth-spirits" inhabited trees and rocks, which became the objects of cult worship. Often a special stone called a *masseba*, was erected for cult worship. Tribal chieftains and their priests in the larger towns encouraged such nonsensical beliefs as the bulwarks of their authority over the terrorized, superstitious population.

Throughout the Middle East, including Arabia, there flourished the worship of insidious female goddesses, overpowering mother-figures who became the object of neurotic devotion. All of these goddesses descended from the Great Mother cults of the Roman Empire era, such as Isis, Artemis, Aphrodite, and Cybele. In Arabia, the chief mother goddess—represented by a stone—was Allat. She was all-powerful, especially among the oligarchical merchant elite of the city of Mecca in western Arabia, and she squatted smilingly over her herd of Bedouin followers, the infantile masses.

Mohammed's revolution not only overthrew the Meccan oligarchy and its goddesses; it revolutionized culture and science. The primary commitment of Mohammed was to the most rapid possible uplifting of the souls of the Arabian population out of their misery and backwardness. He had a mission for them—but first they must learn to read and write, to wage modern war, and to assimilate all the learning of human history for application in rebuilding society.

The Koran, the holy book of Islam, demanded that the Muslims read:

> Recite! In the name of the lord who created,
> Who created men fom clotted blood.
> Recite! Your lord is the most beneficent,
> Who taught by the pen,
> Taught to men what they did not know.

That was the battle cry of Islam. Until that time, written Arabic did not really even exist. Through the circulation of the Koran, an entire section of the world was taught to read and to use the written word.

The message of the Koran was a message of Perfection. Mohammed preached that God has an unshakeable plan for the salvation of mankind. In the Koran, Mohammed makes frequent reference to the destruction of past civilizations, whose bare columns and crumbling ruins could be seen strewn throughout the Near East. Profoundly moved by the collapse of previously great civilizations, Mohammed sought to build an empire that would endure forever, in the realm of ideas. His ideas were incorporated in the famous Constitution of Medina, whose principles included a condemnation of slavery, an attack on the prevalent practice of infanticide, the abolition of usury, the advocacy of a patrilinear rather than a matrilinear society, and rules for commerce and business.

Armed with the Koran, Mohammed's followers established a worldwide empire. For the first time since Alexander the Great, the power of the reactionary feudal Persian oligarchy had been broken. The Mediterranean world was united with central Asia to form an immense, unprecedented common market. The artificial trade barriers that had divided Persia from Byzantium came to an end. Trade flourished, cities grew, and in the next 200 years astonishing scientific and technological breakthroughs were made in agricultural techniques, metals, engineering, and energy technology, beginning with the windmill and the water wheel.

From the start, the new Arab empire drew on every possible source for the scientific and cultural knowledge of the known world. As early as 720 A.D.—and especially under the Golden Age of Caliph Harun al-Rashid and Caliph Mamun until 833 A.D., missions were sent to Athens and Constantinople to secure Greek works that were then quickly translated into Arabic. Learned astronomers of Persia and Egypt were sponsored in new discoveries and record-keeping. Christian physicians began inquiries into the working of the human body and mind. Mathematical science from India and the East flowed into the Muslim world through a dozen different channels, and the civilization of northwest India, long a center of humanism and science, contributed mightily to the Persian renaissance sparked by the merchant Barmakid family of Merv, under the influence of Islam.

All of this came together to establish the great

Abbasid Empire that founded the city of Baghdad in 754. Baghdad was constructed to be the "perfect city" by the universalizing Islamic reformers of the Abbasid movement.

But even before the decline of the Abbasid Empire, the cultish undercurrent of pre-Islamic Arabia persisted. Its patrons were the great merchant oligarchy of Mecca, under the Abu Sofian family and others, who—although they formally surrendered to Mohammed's Islam—never accepted the Koran's tenets. They were the "Muslims who are not Muslims." Covertly, they maintained an alliance against Islam with the Byzantine priesthood, its officials in Egypt and Syria, and the Manichean cult of Persia.

Before the rise of Islam, the Abu Sofian family had sponsored the cult worship of the Meccan goddess Allat. With the decline of the Abbasid Empire, this faction's descendants launched a persecution to stamp out all toleration for new ideas, for science, and for national inquiry. The Caliph Mutawakkil, a puppet caliph installed by the military, summoned a committee of ultra-conservative legal scholars to draft a program for a stifling brand of "orthodoxy." All of a sudden, dozens of schools and scientific centers were shut down, as fundamentalist preachers crisscrossed the empire to stifle all freedom of thought.

Mutawakkil led mass uprisings, not unlike those of the Ayatollah Khomeini's followers, against the rationalist movement of Islam. Raging Bedouins plundered Christian monasteries, Jews and Christians were mass murdered to placate the "orthodox" fanatics, along with many Muslims suddenly condemned for "unorthodox" beliefs. In less than fifty years, the civilization that had taken 200 years to construct was gutted and destroyed, leaving only a few pockets of learning and free inquiry. The evil priesthood-oligarchy alliance had managed to smash one of humanity's treasures.

The man who bears the greatest responsibility for the destruction of education and science in the latter half of the ninth century was Abu al-Hasan Ali bin Ismail al-Ashari. Al-Ashari, the founder of the so-called Asharite school of orthodoxy in Islam, argued that God determines all actions and events arbitrarily. Fire does not burn, he said. God simply causes things to burn when placed in fire. Mohammed's God of Reason was replaced with a capricious, insane god reminiscent of the cult goddesses overthrown by the Prophet Mohammed centuries earlier.°

Al-Ashari's maxim was: "God is free to do good or evil as he chooses."

"Destroy, destroy, destroy. There cannot be destruction enough," the Ayatollah Khomeini told the people of Iran in August 1980. It is an order that goes back to the eleventh-century leveler of the Islamic Renaissance—Al-Ghazali—whose most famous work was called, literally, *Destruction.*

More than any other Muslim philosopher or theologian, the nineteenth-century British Islam specialists studied the work of Al-Ghazali—to use it in creating the

---

° The humanist tradition in Islam did not disappear with the ninth-century victory of the Asharite heresy, however. The tradition of Islamic science and philosophy has been dealt with extensively in the work of Criton Zoakos, editor-in-chief of the *Executive Intelligence Review,* in that magazine and in *The Campaigner* journal.

desired "cult of backwardness" that became the Muslim Brotherhood. Like Al-Ashari, Al-Ghazali argued that the world is essentially irrational, and that human reason cannot be applied to understand the universe and shape its development. In his most famous work *Tahafut al-Falasifah (The Destruction of the Philosophers)*, Al-Ghazali pictured God not as a positive creative force accessible to humanity, but as a remote, arbitrary master. Al-Ghazali is known for his theory of atoms, according to which the universe is composed of an infinite number of discrete particles, each of which, said Al-Ghazali, owes its minute-to-minute existence to the whim of Al-Ghazali's god, who constantly created, destroyed, and then recreated—at every moment—each atom in the entire universe.

In such a universe, governed by no permanence or cause, man's reason is useless; the intellect becomes a dangerous faculty. For Al-Ghazali, as for Aristotle, man is or must be made to be a creature of sense-perception alone, a beastlike, grasping infantile creature incapable of divine reason. In the introduction to his *Destruction*, Al-Ghazali scorns the philosophers and compares them unfavorably to the "unsophisticated masses":

"Now I have observed that there is a class of men who believe in their superiority to others because of their greater intelligence and insight. . . . Such a scandalous attitude is never taken by the unsophisticated masses of men, for they have an instinctive aversion to following the example of misguided genius. Surely, their simplicity is nearer to salvation than sterile genius can be. *For total blindness is less dangerous than oblique vision.*

"Thus, when I saw this vein of folly pulsating among

these idiots, I decided to write this book in order to refute the ancient philosophers. It will expose the incoherence of their beliefs and the inconsistency of their metaphysical theories."

Between the eleventh and fourteenth centuries, the work of Al-Ghazali spread like a foul plague infecting Islam's cities. The vast majority of the Muslim humanist movement was crushed by the tide of reaction and orthodox theology. This is the period that is generally referred to as the "decline of Islamic civilization."

The political-religious base for Al-Ghazali's movement, which took his heresy to every corner of the Muslim world, was the Sufi movement. The Sufis were a loosely organized federation of anti-urban, mystical cultists that were hammered into a powerful force in the years after the destroyer's death. The kinship between Al-Ghazali and the Sufis is even etymological: The word *sufi* is derived from the Arabic *suf,* which means "wool," while the name Al-Ghazali means "the spinner," or one who works with wool.

Even Sufis will admit that Sufism dates back to pre-Islamic times. According to Professor Margaret Smith of Cambridge University, in her *The Way of the Mystics: The Early Christian Mystics and the Rise of the Sufis,* published in 1978 by Oxford University Press, there is a "relationship between the rise and development of a mystical element in Islam—that which we know as Sufism—and the mysticism which was already to be found within the Christian Church of the Near and Middle East at the time when the Arab power established itself." Professor Smith, until her death a British cult specialist, explains that Sufism is the heir not only of

Christian mysticism or "the true Gnostic," but also of the "mystery-cults of the Greeks."

Other scholars have shown conclusively that Christian gnosticism—as a cult heresy within the early Church—is itself derived from the Oriental cults and mystery religions of the ancient East. The definitive work on this subject is *The Gnostic Religion* by Hans Jonas, who proves that the Oriental cults that later emerged as the gnostic movement "compounded everything—oriental mythologies, astrological doctrines, Iranian theology, elements of the Jewish tradition, whether Biblical, rabbinical, or occult, Christian salvation-eschatology, and Platonic terms and constructs." It is this eclectic religious tradition embodied in gnosticism that, after the rise of Islam, was born again as Sufism. The goddess Allat and her cult followers of Mecca were the transmission belt for these ancient Eastern heresies.

Yet modern Sufis like to pride themselves on Sufism's indefinable nature. In *The Sufis*, Sufi scholar Idris Shah, writes: "According to one Persian scholar, Sufism is a Christian aberration. A professor at Oxford thinks that it is influenced by the Hindu Vedanta. An Arab-American professor speaks of it as a reaction against intellectualism in Islam. A professor of Semitic literature claims traces of central Asian Shamanism. A German will have us find in it Christianity plus Buddhism. Two very great English Orientalists put their money on a strong Neoplatonic influence; yet, one of them will concede that it was perhaps independently generated. . . ." And so on.

How does Idris Shah define Sufism? "A Sufi is a Sufi."

But then Idris Shah cites Ishan Naiser, another Sufi, to define the cult: "I am the pagan; I worship at the altar of the Jew; I am the idol of the Yemenite, the actual temple of the fire-worshippers; the priest of the Magian; the inner reality of the cross-legged Brahmin meditating; the brush and color of the artist; the suppressed, powerful personality of the scoffer. . . . When a flame is thrown into another flame, they join at the point of flameness.' "

Idris Shah, now a resident in London where he works with the Muslim Brotherhood, epitomizes the Sufi cult in its modern form. Passing himself off as a scholar of Sufism and the Islamic religion, he is the author of several rather queer works, including the famous *Book of the Book*, a 250-page volume of blank pages that contains a mystical "message." The book, like the modern cult, is a fraud.

Upon the death of Al-Ghazali, the Sufi mystic Ibn al-Arabi became the official father of Islamic mysticism from the twelfth century onward. The object of Sufism, according to Ibn al-Arabi, is to find the "intermediate world" in which direct communication between man and God is possible. This, Ibn al-Arabi said, is the "world of the imagination." In the Sufi view, this world of dreams and fantasies is described as "illumination." It is often reached with the aid of hallucinogenic drugs that can induce the "heavenly vision."

Like some oriental cults such as Zen Buddhism, the Sufis believe in seeking a merger between man's consciousness and God's. These ecstatic movements have given rise over the years to the many transcendental orders of mystics and dervishes, many of whom are still in existence today. Among the chief ones are the Qadiri, the Naqshbandi, and the Suhrawardi. In the Sufi tradition, any important leader of a group de facto creates his own sub-order, leading to a constant proliferation of Sufi orders.

Over the centuries and still today, Sufism is devoted

to the worship of the grave and death. Tombs and burial sites are shrines for followers of Sufism. Many of the Sufi traditions, as holdovers from pre-Islamic times, have introduced pagan rites and rituals into the quasi-Islamic ceremonies of the Sufis. Witchcraft and other such devil worship and mother-goddess worship are common in Sufi circles, though disguised, along with magic and incantations.

It is the Sufi heresy that became the vehicle for the penetration of British imperialism into the Middle East.

Beginning as early as the seventeenth century, the British aristocracy had established numbers of centers for political intelligence on the Muslim world. With the gradual expansion of the British Empire through the East India Company and the Levant Company, the British found themselves in regular contact with the Muslim populations of the Near East and India.

To the British, Muslim tendencies that fostered the growth of natural science or that encouraged powerful monarchies within the Islamic world were potential danger to the Empire. To ensure London's domination of the "subject races," the British imperial strategists sought out currents within the Muslim world that cohered with the British interest in preventing progress. Rather than deal with kings and princes who ruled over wide areas, the British also encouraged the power of hundreds of tribal and ethnic groups, each to rule over a small mini-state. In this way, the British would more easily prevent the emergence of political opposition to their rule. The American Revolution was enough, the British believed.

Tightly organized but divided along tribal and other lines, the Sufis were the perfect partner for the British colonialists. Because of their antipathy to science, the Sufis would not present difficult demands for the spread of industrial revolution to India and the Middle East; they would be content to be cotton growers, tea pickers, and so forth. Having determined how useful Sufi mysticism could be, the British encouraged its spread and funded missionary and proselytizing campaigns by Sufi preachers.

From the alliance with Sufism during the eighteenth century, it was only a short step during the nineteenth century for the British to sponsor the creation of cults and pseudo-religions as a tool of Empire policy. Having carefully studied the Roman Empire as their model, the British had concluded that one of the chief reasons the Roman oligarchy had survived for 1,000 years was because it had learned how to use cults and "religions" to control its people.

During the 1820s the British oligarchy established the so-called Oxford Movement, a groundswell of religious reform fever organized by Oxford University, the Anglican Church, and Kings College of London University. Their movement created a special kind of British "missionary," whose task it was to spread the perverted gospel of the Oxford Movement into other parts of the world.

The umbrella for this movement was not a church, but the Scottish Rite of Freemasonry.

The missionaries of the Oxford Movement were assigned to build subsidiary branches of the Scottish Rite throughout the Empire. When approaching an area like the Middle East, the Oxford Movement's freemasonic evangelists would not attempt to convert Muslims, for instance, to Christianity. Instead, they would try to bring the Muslim (Sufi) belief system into harmony with the cult practices of the Scottish Rite. Because of their highly heterodox, cult beliefs, the Scottish freemasons were bitterly condemned by the Catholic Church as an anti-religious conspiracy capable of undercutting the authority of the Pope within the Church.

The Oxford Movement and the British freemasons had an ally that had also been condemned by the Vatican: the Society of Jesus, or the Jesuits. The Anglo-Jesuit alliance still stands today as the centerpiece of the European nobility's dark ages plot.

The chief sponsors of the British cult-building project during this period were the British royal family itself and many of its leading prime ministers and aides, such as Benjamin Disraeli, Lord Palmerston, Lord Shaftesbury, and Edward Bulwer-Lytton. From the 1820s onward, the British aristocracy was ruled by a clique of the most degenerate, sexually perverse, and evil men and women the world has known. For their model, they took the image of the monstrous cult center that was Pompeii, in ancient Rome, where animal worship and bestiality were the rule of "civilized" behavior.

Bulwer-Lytton, who served as the head of Britain's Colonial Office and India Office for years and then was succeeded by his son, was a practicing member of the ancient cult of Isis and Osiris, a death cult of Egypt under the late pharaohs that spread its poison throughout the Mediterranean world in the years before the coming of Christianity. In his cult novel *The Last Days of Pompeii*, Bulwer-Lytton set the foundation for the cults of future generations. This paragon of the empire-builder is the grandfather of the Pre-Raphaelite Brotherhood of John Ruskin, the 1860s Metaphysical Society of Bertrand Russell, the 1880s Isis-Urania Temple of the Golden Dawn of Aldous Huxley, and the Theosophy Society of Madame Blavatsky, who published *Isis Unveiled*. Rites of black magic, devil worship, and self-multilation were a common feature of the British aristocracy during this period. Jack the Ripper was the most degenerate product of this cult life. His gruesome murders of whores in London's streets were part of a cult ritual!

The first recorded project of the nineteenth-century British cult aristocracy was the movement of the Bahais in Persia. Although it began as an experimental British foray in nonreligious, freemasonic cults, the Bahai movement would spawn the organizer of the future pan-Islamic movement—Jamaleddine Al-Afghani.

The Bahai cult was founded in approximately 1844 by a missionary named Miza Husayn Ali. He called himself Bahaullah. Today, the Bahais number over 300,000 in Iran alone, although many of them have quietly fled since the arrival of Khomeini's regime. But if their largest number is in Iran, the largest Bahai temple is in Haifa, Israel, and the world headquarters of the organization is in Wilmette, Illinois.

Bahaiism began as a radical messianic cult in Persia that claimed to be a new religion and drew on a mishmash of Muslim, Christian, Zoroastrian, and Jewish ideas. The Bahais argued that their new doctrine superseded all other religions in a "one world faith." Although they preached love and universal brotherhood, they quickly found themselves most unwelcome throughout Persia and the Middle East, for the Bahais became known as religious fanatics who were willing to do anything to further the cause of their faith. In 1852,

a Bahai leader was arrested after he tried to assassinate
the Shah of Persia. The Bahais were suppressed in Persia,
and many of their top leaders rounded up and exiled,
first to Baghdad and then to Constantinople.

During this time the Bahai leaders—then including
Bahaullah and his son, Abdul-Baha—maintained close
ties to both the British Scottish Rite and to a proliferation
of branch temples and movements spreading into India,
the Ottoman Empire, Russia, and even Africa. In 1868,
the Turkish government decided that it was too dangerous for the Bahais to be allowed to function freely, and
they were placed under house arrest in Acre, in Syria.
But, with their powerful friends in London, the Bahai
clique always managed to surface again.

By the 1890s, the cult was again gathering momen-
tum, especially in Persia. E. G. Browne, a British cult
specialist who studied Persia, went so far as to proclaim
that the Bahais were the wave of the future in the
Mideast. The British administrator in Egypt, Lord Curzon, declared that if they maintained their pace, the
Bahais might "replace" Islam as the dominant religion
in Persia!

By the first years of the twentieth century, it was
common knowledge that the Bahai was a product of
British inspiration. They were accused by the Turkish
government of trying to establish a pseudotribal "col-
ony" in Syria as a beachhead for the British in the
Ottoman Empire. In 1904 and again in 1907, the Turks
investigated the Bahais, and the investigation's report
recommended that they be banished from the Empire.
Before the sentence could be carried out, however, the
so-called Young Turks—another fifth column of the
Scottish Rite of Freemasonry and the Grand Orient

Lodge—seized power in their revolution. Abdul-Baha was released from prison.

After his release, the Bahai leader went to London and New York, where he met the elite of both cities. In 1912, he set out on a speaking tour of the United States where, according to the official Bahai publications, he spoke to "university students, socialists, Mormons, Jews, Christians, agnostics, Esperantists, peace societies, New Thought clubs, women's suffrage societies," and many other centers.

In 1918, Abdul-Baha was knighted by the Queen of England.

Everywhere he went, he preached a single message: the necessity of abolishing nation-states, existing world religions, and national borders to melt everything into a single world order. The Bahai cult took a leading role in the founding of the World League of Nations, the forerunner of the United Nations, and his organization had close ties to the World Federalists. Abdul-Baha's daughter married the founder of the so-called Esperanto language, a project to abolish all tongues and replace them with one language. The Bahais could also be found in the middle of the British-led social reform movements.

Today the Bahai cult is hated in Iran, and is considered correctly to be an arm of the British Crown. During the destabilization of the Shah in 1978, it was widely reported that in several instances the Bahai cult secretly funded the Khomeini Shiite movement. In part, the money would have flowed through the cult's links to the same international "human rights" organizations, such as Amnesty International, that originally sponsored the anti-Shah movement in Iran. These movements also derive from the "one world" currents associated with the

Bahais since the early 1900s. (If any Iranians have been misled on the question of the Bahais by the supposed antipathy of Khomeini's clique to the Bahais, it should be noted that the Bahai cultists often deliberately encouraged anti-Bahai activities as camouflage.)

"You have made us with your hands, invested our matter with its perfect form, and created us in the best shape. Through you we have known the whole universe," said a disciple of Al-Afghani, the British agent who organized the first pan-Islamic fundamentalist movement.

Jamaleddin al-Afghani was born, according to most accounts, somewhere in central Asia—probably in Kabul, Afghanistan. His early years are now lost in obscurity, although there are some reports that he was born a Jew and that he very early entered the ranks of one of the many Sufi brotherhoods that covered that part of Asia.

Because of the close ties between central Asia and India, many of the Sufi cults were based in India or derived from missionaries spreading Sufism out of Indian Muslim circles. The most important was the Naqshbandi sect. The name means "enemies of laughter." The Naqshbandi sect grew rapidly as a central Asian Sufi brotherhood at the beginning of the 1700s under Sheikh Ahmed Sirhindi and then Shah Waliullah of Delhi, his successor, who lived from 1703 to 1765. Both of these Sufi mystics arose to preach an ultra-orthodox ideology and a return to "pure Islam" after the collapse of the Mogol Empire in India and the decline of Islam in the East.

Naqshbandi teachers traveled from Central Asia to Mecca, Cairo, Turkey, and Persia spreading the Sufi mystical revival. The son of Shah Waliullah, Shah Abdel-Aziz, gathered around him a network of disciples including the Kurdish Sheikh Khalid al-Baghdadi (1775-1826), who visited India in 1809. Radiating from Indian centers where the British Colonial Office ruled, Eastern mysticism engendered a revival of xenophobic, Islamic "purity" that considered all outside influences as suspect and evil. Some of the Islamic orders demanded that all Muslims "safeguard ourselves from the penetration of Persian traditions and Indian habits." Among the movements that arose during this period were the extremist Wahhabi movement in the Arabian peninsula and the North African cult called the "Senussi Brotherhood," based in Libya.

From 1857 until his death in 1897, Al-Afghani was the chief standard-bearer of the fundamentalist movement that embraced the Sufis, the Bahais, and the freemasons.

Throughout his forty-year career as a British intelligence agent, Al-Afghani was guided by two British Islamic and cult specialists, Wilfrid Scawen Blunt and Edward G. Browne. E. G. Browne was Britain's leading Orientalist of the nineteenth century, and could number among his protégés at Cambridge University's Orientalist department the young Harry St.-John B. Philby, the British intelligence specialist in the Arabian peninsula and father of the MI-6 "triple agent," Kim Philby.

Like Philby and T. E. Lawrence later, Browne cultivated a studied pose as an "anti-imperialist," who would loudly voice his criticism of British policies toward its colonies. He claimed to be sympathetic to the aspirations of independence movements. A dedicated cultist, he admitted to to a fascination with Oriental mysticism and the "sacred mysteries of the East." His specialty was the study of Sufism and the Bahai cult, an interest that was apparently sparked by the work of a fanatical French Jesuit idologue named Joseph de Gobineau.

Gobineau was a French diplomat who exhibited a strong love for the British, and it was his work—particularly his book *Philosophy in Central Asia*—that inspired the cultist yearnings of such figures as British Prime Minister Benjamin Disraeli. Gobineau was recruited to the British SIS in Switzerland and was subsequently posted to Iran in the French foreign service. There he spent most of his time in the southern Iranian city of Shiraz, the city out of which the Bahai cult first emerged. Gobineau's chief preoccupation was to assemble a working partnership between the Aryan and Semitic races, including the allegedly Aryan Persians. (Later, he would become one of the forefathers of the Nazi movement out of his advocacy of "race science.") Years later, E. G. Browne described with reverence how he first learned of Gobineau's work:

"One day some seven years ago I was searching amongst the books of the University of Cambridge library for fresh materials for an essay on Sufi philosophy," wrote Browne, "when my eye caught the title of Count de Gobineau's work *Religion and Philosophy in Central Asia.* I took down the book, glanced through it to discover whether or not it contained any account of the Sufis, and finding a short chapter was devoted to them, brought it back with me to my room. My first superficial glance had also shown me that a considerable portion of the book was taken up with an account of the Bahais. . . ."

He continued: "When, however, I turned from this mournful chapter to that portion of the book dealing with the Bahai movement, the case was altogether different. To anyone who has already read this masterpiece of historical description. . . . It is needless to describe the effect which it produced on me. I had long ardently wanted to visit Persia and above all Shiraz, and this desire was now greatly intensified. I now wished to see it because it was the birthplace of Mirza Ali Muhammed the Bab [founder of the Bahai]."

In 1887, Browne did visit Persia, and became probably the world's authority on that country, writing the classic *Persian Revolution* and *A Year Among the Persians*. The man who taught Persian to Browne was Mirza Mohammed Baqir, one of Al-Afghani's associates in the Persian cult of the Bahai. Baqir has been described as "successively a Shiite, a Muhammedan, a dervish, a Christian, an atheist, and a Jew," who finished his travels "by elaborating a religious system of his own which he called 'Islamo-Christianity.' "

Baqir had been recruited into the inner circle of the Persian and Central Asian elite that would be the founding members of the pan-Islamic movement by Wilfrid S. Blunt, another member of the British Orientalist school, who was given the responsibility by the Scottish Rite of Freemasons to organize the Persian and and Middle East "lodges." The movement's driving force would be Al-Afghani.

Al-Afghani's career began in earnest in 1870, when he took up a position with the Board of Education in Istanbul, Turkey. Earlier Al-Afghani had been involved in Central Asian politics and, for a time, had served as prime minister of Afghanistan in 1866, where he maintained ties to the Bahais, the British masons, and certain Sufis based in India. In 1869, he went to India, and from there traveled to Istanbul. During his days in Turkey, Al-Afghani was intensely disliked by the clergy of the Muslim establishment there. After but a short time he was expelled from Turkey for preaching doctrines considered by the *ulema* to be hostile to Islam. (Only two years earlier, the Turkish government had also arrested the leadership of the Bahai cult. Forced to leave Istanbul, Afghani went to Cairo, where he remained for nine years.)

Beginning in 1871 in Cairo, Afghani was sponsored by none other than Prime Minister Mustafa Riad Pasha, who had met him in Istanbul, and who made sure that Afghani was placed on a generous cash stipend and given a position at the famous Muslim university of Al Azhar. Chastened by his experience in Istanbul, and quietly warned by his British patrons not to become too rambunctious right away, for seven years Afghani maintained strict Muslim orthodoxy in his public teaching, while privately building up a cult following. Finally, in 1878, Afghani left Al Azhar and moved into the Jewish Quarter of Cairo, where he began open political organizing.

Afghani announced the formation of the Arab Masonic Society. With the help of Riad Pasha and London's embassy in Cairo, Afghani reorganized the Scottish Rite and Grand Orient lodges of freemasons in Cairo. He began to organize around him a web of several Muslim countries, especially Syria, Turkey, and Persia.

Among his followers, Afghani received almost total devotion bordering on idolatry. His most prized disciple was Mohammed Abduh, who, long after Afghani left Cairo, organized the basis for Hasan al-Banna's Muslim Brotherhood.

In his work *Treatise of Mystical Inspirations*, Abduh described his encounter with Afghani: "While I found myself in this state, the arrival of the perfect Sage, of Truth personified, of our venerated master Sayyid Jamal ad-Din al-Afghani who does not cease to garner the fruits of science, made the sun of truths rise for us which illuminated the most complicated problem." Such language—"perfect Sage" and "Truth personified"—is reserved only for use by Sufi mystics.

While still in Cairo, Afghani was involved in the founding meetings of several Middle East secret societies. Addressing Syrian Christians in Alexandria, he delivered a panegyric on his vision of the future of the Arab world. The group was reportedly so inspired by Afghani's sermon that it prevailed upon Syrian and Egyptian Muslims to form a movement that became known as "Young Egypt," or *Misr al-Fatat*. This secret society, which lasted well into the twentieth century and still has adherents today, was a proto-Nazi organization of fanatical Egyptian nationalists long controlled by the Scottish Rite of Freemasons. Likewise, Afghani was involved in the creation of another masonic cult, the so-called Young Turks, the mystical society that, in 1908, seized control briefly of the Ottoman Empire. A third spinoff of Afghani's work in Egypt was the formation of the Syrian nationalist secret societies. Each one of these movements was established as a project of the British SIS.

In 1879, he was expelled from Egypt with an official state document that accused him of having formed a "secret society" of "young thugs" to bring the "ruin of religion and of rule." But it was too late: in 1882, Afghani's movement organized the cult rebellion of

Arabi in Egypt, which launched an agent provocateur
revolt against the British *khedive* who had expelled
Afghani. The revolt provided the pretext for the British
armed invasion and occupation of Egypt. In Egypt, at
least, Afghani had been successful!

From Egypt, Afghani visited India briefly and then
went to Europe. With financing from the British in
Egypt, Afghani established a French-language journal
and an Arabic journal in Paris called *Al-Urwah al-Wuthkah* ("The Indissoluble Bond"), which was also the name
of a secret organization he had founded in 1883. *The
Indissoluble Bond is the direct forerunner of the Muslim
Brotherhood.*

It was the first real pan-Islamic organization. Its
purpose, said Afghani, was "to unite Muslims and arouse
them from the sleep and acquaint them with the dangers
threatening them and guide them to the way of meeting
these dangers." Among the members of Afghani's Paris
circle there were Egyptians, Indians, Turks, Syrians,
North Africans, as well as many Christians and Jews! A
parallel organization, called *Umm al-Kurah* was established by Afghani's followers in Mecca, but it was
quickly suppressed.

Among the Paris associates in 1884 we find:

Malkam Khan, an Armenian Christian who converted to the Shiite Muslim faith, and who became the
Persian ambassador to London during the 1880s. Malkam Khan's father Yakub Khan was the founder of the
Scottish Rite of Freemasons in Persia and a close associate of Blunt.

Mirza Muhammed Baqir, another freemason, who
was E. G. Browne's Persian-language instructor, and
who had invented "Islamo-Christianity."

Reverend Louis Sabunji, a Catholic priest of North Mesopatamia, who converted to Islam and became the personal secretary to Wilfrid Blunt.

Adib Ishaq, a Syrian Christian freemason, who was a writer and a radical anticleric who condemned the Catholic and Maronite clergy of the Middle East in his works.

James Sanua, an Egyptian Jew who taught Afghani French, who founded a journal dedicated to the principle that all religions must be subsumed in a single "religion of humanity."

And many Persian Bahais gathered under Afghani's umbrella after having been driven out of the Middle East.

What strikes even the casual observer about this group is that very few of them were even Muslims, and virtually every one had a background of involvement in the "universal religion" movement. They hardly seem to be the collection of people appropriate to create an pan-Islamic movement. And Al-Afghani, whose frequent assertions of his own belief in the "unity of the three religions" and other cult nonsense of the Bahai variety were anything but the views of a fanatical Muslim, hummed a different tune in the pages of *Al-Urwah al-Wuthkah*. England, wrote Al-Afghani, cannot hope to "stifle the voice of the *Mahdi* (Muslim savior), the most awesome of all voices since its power is even greater than the Voice of Holy War, which issues from all Muslim mouths."

Continued Afghani: "Does England think herself able to stifle this voice before it makes itself heard in all the East from Mount Himalaya to Dawlaghir, from north to south, speaking to the Muslims of Afghanistan, of Sind and of India, proudly proclaiming the coming of the Savior whom every son of Islam awaits with such impatience. *El-Mahdi, El-Mahdi, El-Mahdi.*"

The impact of the *Al-Urwah al-Wuthkah*, though brief in duration, was enormous in its scope. Instantly, Afghani became the voice of the pan-Islamic movement. A hundred different cults, previously scattered across the Muslim world without a leader, began to come together under one single command. Secret societies flourished now in Syria, Egypt, Turkey, Persia, and India, not isolated as before, but conscious in the knowledge that they were part of a unified movement. And, although Afghani loudly denounced the British in almost every breath, he was a consummate agent for the British— using London as the lightning rod for the various Muslim extremist cults.

In a letter to Wilfrid Blunt, Malkam Khan described his method: "I went to Europe and studied there the religious, social, and political systems of the West. I learned the spirit of the various sects of Christianity and the organization of the secret societies and freemasons, and I conceived a plan which should incorporate the political wisdom of Europe with the religious wisdom of Asia. I knew that it was useless to attempt a remodeling of Persia in European forms and I was determined to clothe my material reformation in a garb which my people would understand, the garb of religion." In just a few years, the "remodeling" of Persia would occur with an explosion of violence in the 1905 Revolution. It would be almost an exact replica of the revolution of 1978-1979.

In 1885, Afghani traveled to Russia and then Persia, where he was asked by the Shah Nasir ad-Din to become prime minister. Nasir ad-Din had been ruling Persia for over forty years, and there is little doubt that he would not have asked Afghani to become prime minister without prompting from the British. One year later, in 1890, he ordered Afghani to leave the country. The pan-Islamic leader fled to London. There, together with Malkam Khan—who resigned, finally, as Persia's ambassador in London—Afghani organized a political destabilization of Iran beginning in 1891. Afghani and Khan accused the Shah of persecuting men of religion and whipped up Shiite radicalism against the Persian king; once, to emphasize the "Islamic character" of his movement, Afghani signed his name Sayyed al-Hussaini, to imply that he himself was descended from the Prophet! The Shah several times officially protested to the British government about Afghani's activities, but the British said only that they could not control the actions of a private individual. Finally, in 1895, one of Al-Afghani's close associates assassinated Shah Nasir ad-Din.

Once, Afghani was explicit about his connections to the British Empire. During an 1884 visit to London, he reportedly made an astonishing proposal to the British: If London would withdraw from the Sudan, where rebels in the Nile Valley were battling the British occupation, then Afghani would arrange for a British-sponsored military pact with Turkey, Persia, and Afghanistan against Russia!

In 1897, Afghani died. But the movement that he had founded under the banner of pan-Islamicism did not die. It would continue to spread like some pestilence through the next century.

To see how it took root, we must now turn to Egypt—and the founding of the Muslim Brotherhood.

March, 1980: Zbigniew Brzezinski on trip to Pakistan to propose military alliance with Zia regime.

Treason in the U.S.

Billy Carter learns strategy from official of Qaddafi regime in Libya, another country where U.S. embassy was burned in late 1979.

November, 1979: Pakistani army helicopter hovers over U.S. embassy, burned by "Islamic fundamentalist" mob with tacit encouragement of Zia's government.

U.S. Navy's Office of Naval Research building in Washington, D.C., where Khomeini's espionage agent Capt. Siavash Setoudeh maintained office complex for months after hostage seizure.

Washington, D.C. rug dealership front for Bahram Nahidian—Savama chief in U.S. under Khomeini, controller of Setoudeh and of Khomeini's "hit teams."

Treason in the U.S.

The arm of the Muslim Brotherhood in the U.S., the Muslim Student Association, holds a national conference in Miami, Ohio in May 1980. The MSA, run top down by the Brotherhood from abroad, is financed from Iran through Bahram Nahidian's networks.

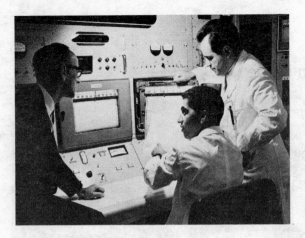

Iran, 1968: Entering nuclear age. Teheran University Nuclear Center visited by International Atomic Energy Agency specialist.

'Pol Pot' in Iran

Iran, 1979: above, frenzied worshippers flagellate themselves near U.S. embassy.

Iran, 1980: Khomeini's social structure—(right) back to the 12th century "Destruction" of al-Ghazali.

Iran, 1980: Heroin addicts (left) in Teheran. In one year Iran and Pakistan surpassed Southeast Asia as world's primary source of opium.

The 'Radical' Traitors. . .

Bernard Lewis of Princeton University, author of design for breakup of nations of the Middle East. (near right)

Richard Falk at Princeton; key pro-Khomeini organizer in Iran and U.S. (center right)

Ramsey Clark, Carter's link to Khomeini before and after the Shah's fall. (far right)

. . . and 'Establishment' Traitors

U.S. Air Force Gen. Robert E. Huyser, NATO emissary later blamed by many Iranians for undercutting the Shah.

CFR member George Ball (right) coordinated the political side of Huyser's "shift to neutral."

Anthony Blunt, Art Curator to the Queen, visionary of sacerdotal revolutions, sometime "Soviet spy."

The British Operatives

Blunt's boys: Cambridge "Apostles" kooks in 1932.

H.A.R. "Kim" Philby, Blunt's recruit from Cambridge in 1932, now shapes Middle East policy for the KGB.

Historian Arnold Toynbee, British intelligence "thinker" behind Blunt, Philby, et al.

Historic Enemies

Kemal Ataturk, Turkish Republic's nationalist founder, in opposition to whose profound influence the Muslim Brotherhood was founded.

Muslim Brotherhood rounded up in Egypt after 1954 attempt to assassinate Egyptian President Gamel Abdul Nasser.

British Arabist H. St.-John Philby ("Kim" Philby's father) on camel in Arabian desert, 1917.

"Islamic fundamentalism" today: U.S.-trained environmentalist Ibrahim Yazdi (left); fanatic Iranian Prime Minister Rajai (right).

6

Muslim Brotherhood II:
Headquarters
In Egypt

The well-dressed gentlemen have begun to file into the meeting room one by one, each taking his seat and puffing on his pipe or fiddling with his papers awaiting the rest of the assembly. Outside, the London air is taking on its first chill: it is October 29, 1918, and England has been victorious in that unfortunate event called the Great War. Now, there are other pressing matters to attend to. The first to enter the room is Lord Curzon, the ultra-imperialist foreign secretary whose special knowledge of the Middle East will find useful employment today; then the aristocratic Robert Cecil, whose walk reveals that he is conscious of his family's 300-year predominance in English politics; he is quickly followed by his cousin, Arthur Lord Balfour; South Africa's minister of defense General Smuts; Edwin Montague, the secretary of state for India and the only Jew in the room; and Mark Sykes, the Foreign Office's Middle East genius. At the end of the parade is an impressive delegation from military intelligence.

Lord Curzon speaks first. "What is to be done, I say, about this deplorable agreement to which the French seem disposed to adhere most tenaciously?" he asks. Curzon is speaking of the Sykes-Picot Agreement, which was agreed upon secretly in 1916 between London and Paris, according to whose most regrettable provisions London then agreed to bequeath Syria and Lebanon to France at the end of the war.

T. E. Lawrence enters the room. Although he is not an aristocrat, Lawrence is not fazed by the awesome combination of British nobility assembled there. For Lawrence has been trained by and for the aristocracy: classical studies at Oxford University, personal training in intelligence by Dr. David George Hogarth, author, archaeologist, Orientalist, and keeper of the Ashmolean Museum at Oxford. That was many years ago; since the war D. G. Hogarth had been named to head the prestigious Arab Bureau of British Military Intelligence in Cairo, where he took Lawrence under his wing. Now, Lawrence had come from Cairo to explain to the assembled gentlemen his strategy for dealing with the French.

Lawrence, thinks Curzon, is an amateur. Cecil, Curzon, and the rest have already decided to appoint Arnold Toynbee to head the special task force to oversee British dismantling of the Ottoman Empire. But right now the French business presents a more pressing puzzle. Working alongside Toynbee will be Winston Churchill, who, Curzon thinks to himself with a bit of annoyance, seems to have made the Middle East almost his personal fiefdom. As for Lawrence "of Arabia," he may have been the best field intelligence officer in Britain's secret service these past several years, but he is still a field man. Yet, thinks Curzon, what the man is saying makes sense. Lord Cromer of Egypt and E. G. Browne would be pleased.

"If the Sultan of Turkey were to disappear," T. E. was saying, "then the Caliphate by the common consent of Islam would fall to the family of the prophet, the present representative of which is Hussein, the Sharif of Mecca." He clears his throat. "Hussein's activities seem beneficial to us, because it marches with our immediate aims, the breakup of the Islamic bloc and the disruption of the Ottoman Empire, and because the states he would set up to succeed the Turks would be as harmless to ourselves as Turkey was. If properly handled the Arab States would remain in a state of political mosaic, a tissue of jealous principalities incapable of cohesion, and yet always ready to combine against an outside force."

The council makes a tentative decision to support at least some of Lawrence's plan, and further discussion with the Roundtable will be needed. The meeting is over. The recommendations of Lawrence's Arab Bureau are usually not questioned by Her Majesty's government, and this plan seems to be particularly sound. By dismembering Turkey and, in the process, eliminating the only existing central Muslim authority as represented by the centuries-old caliphate, any possibility that the Germans or the Russians—who seem to have undue political influence in Turkey anyway—will gain control over the political mechanism of Islam will be removed. By the same token, the Arabian tribes of the Hijaz loyal to

Hussein are merely vassals of London's Arab Bureau. With British intelligence in control of the new caliphate, the entire Muslim world will in effect fall under the guidance of the pro-British Meccans.

Great Britain's geopolitical alliance with Islamic fundamentalism is born.

It was not really as easy as all that, of course. Certainly, over the past thirty years Cairo had been transformed into the regional subheadquarters of British intelligence, and a sophisticated operation it was. Out of Cairo, and funded with British gold, the Arab Bureau controlled a dozen different Muslim fundamentalist movements. All they would need was eventual centralization to provide better coordination for tactical changes in British Empire policy. But an absolutely invaluable foundation had been constructed.

Consider the case of the Senussi Brotherhood.

Through the Senussi Brotherhood, headquartered in Cairo, Britain's Arab Bureau had established fortresses of British influence stretching down the deepest recesses of central Africa.

The founder of the Senussi Order of *Ikhwan* (Brothers) was Mohammed bin Ali al-Senussi al-Khattabi al-Idrisi al-Hassani, who was born somewhere in Algeria in the 1780s. Senussi studied at Karuwiyin University in Fez, Morocco, and in 1829 he was moved to found a secret society of Sufi ascetics in the Sahara Desert, modeled on the ancient orders of Christian monks. The movement's slogan was "Islamic unity," and it spread gradually into Tunisia, Tripolitania, and Cyrenaica. (In 1951, Tripolitania and Cyrenaica would unite to form

the state of "Libya.") In a few years, Senussi traveled to
Mecca in Arabia. It was on this voyage that he and his
companions established the "Senussi Brotherhood."

Though it was clearly North African in origin, the
Senussi Brotherhood had a great deal in common with a
similar fundamentalist cult that was gathering adherents
in Arabia: the Wahhabi. Both the Wahhabi and the
Senussi reflected the impact of the orthodox Sufi mystical currents then flowing out of British India.

In 1830, the French invaded Algeria. In response, the
Ottoman Empire invaded Libya again. Senussi traveled
back from Arabia and Yemen, where he now had a
branch of the Brotherhood, to North Africa toward
Algeria. But the French, who apparently believed Senussi to be a dangerous agitator in the pay of the British,
blocked his entry to Algeria, and he was forced to halt in
Libya where he set up his headquarters in Cyrenaica.
There, on the Mediterranean coast near Egypt, Senussi
directed the White Monastery (*Zawiya al-Baida*), which
became the mother lodge of the order. In 1853, he
moved his headquarters south to the oasis village of
Giarabub in the middle of the desert, where he founded
his cultist Islamic University. That monastery sat astride
the old desert Bedouin trade route linking Benghazi to
points in central Africa, including the town of Wadai,
whose Sultan Mohammed Sharif was one of Senussi's old
Meccan allies from the 1820s.

As the years passed, the Order of the Senussis grew.
By 1882, there were thirty-eight *zawiyas* in Cyrenaica,
seventeen in Egypt, eighteen in Tripolitania, with others
scattered across the North African desert. The estimated
total of its adherents was between 1.5 and 3 million
ikhwanis. In its actions, the order was openly anti-
French, and it backed rebels in Algeria against the

French colonialists—while it refused to help the Mahdi of Sudan, who was fighting against Britain's General Charles Gordon at Khartoum in the 1880s. In 1894, the Senussi Order moved its headquarters to the remote oasis of Kufra deep in the Libyan desert. From there the Senussi waged constant war against the French from Algeria and Tunisia to the center of Africa. Mohammed al-Mahdi, Senussi's son and successor, directed guerrilla warfare against the French from a military camp based at Lake Chad.

Until this time, the Senussi Brotherhood was only a minor adjunct of British intelligence operations in the Muslim world. But in 1897 Wilfrid Scawen Blunt took the arduous journey to the Senussi oasis in Africa. During the next twenty years, the British paid an increasing amount of attention to the Senussi movement. In 1916, upon the death of Mohammed al-Mahdi, the young Idris became the chief of the Senussi Brotherhood. In 1951, he would be proclaimed King Idris I of Libya in a United Nations ceremony.

After World War I, the Senussi Brotherhood was formally appropriated as an asset of Britain's Arab Bureau in Cairo, and an eager agent of British intelligence was dispatched to Tripolitania to help organize the order's political work. The agent's name was Abdel-Rahman Azzam. Many years later, he would become the first Secretary-General of the British-sponsored League of Arab States after World War II.

The Senussi Brotherhood was only one among many operations watched over by the Arab Bureau from its command center in Egypt. Of all the Arab countries, Egypt was the only one occupied by British armed forces and governed by a British administrator. Centrally located in the Arab world and by far the most populous Arab country, Egypt sat astride the vital Suez Canal that was the lifeline of the British Empire and the transit point for its naval bases from Gibraltar, Malta, Crete, and Cyprus in the Mediterranean into the Indian Ocean and "east of Suez."

British aristocrats had long been fascinated with Egypt's history, especially with the mysteries of the ancient Egypt of the pyramids and pharoahs. The Scottish Rite Freemasons were obsessed with its age-old cults and the temple of Jerusalem, which both figure prominently in the mystical rites of the British masonic societies. For men like Cecil, Curzon, and Lord Cromer, Egypt's mystique held an almost overpowering attraction.

Since al-Afghani's stay in Cairo between 1871 and 1879, the British SIS and the Oxford and Cambridge Orientalists had made of Egypt a bustling headquarters for Afghani's movement. Afghani had held court to delegations of Syrian Orthodox and Greek Orthodox Arab Christians from Lebanon and Alexandria, Egypt; of Libyan desert tribal chieftains and African Muslim sultans; of Lebanese Maronite warlords; of Arabian sheikhs and Sufi mystics from Persia and Afghanistan; and of obscure Indian Muslim cults and secret societies. But more than anything else, Afghani—and England's intelligence service—had captured Egypt's soul. Under the careful hand of Lord Cromer, a scion of the famous Baring banking family who was the lord of Egypt before World War I, Egypt's emerging national elite was infected with the poison of Islamic fanaticism, British liberalism, and Egyptian cult revivalism. It is a poison of which, almost exactly 100 years later, the Egyptian nation has yet to purge itself.

Egypt was also the home of Afghani's most stalwart disciple, Mohammed Abduh.

In 1871, when Afghani arrived in Cairo to take his position at Al Azhar University, Mohammed Abduh gravitated around Afghani's inner circle. Though only in his early twenties and much younger than Afghani, he became his master's closest collaborator and, when Afghani was made to leave Egypt in 1879, Abduh followed him to London and Paris a few years later.

Abduh's life had been one of almost total immersion in the Sufi cult. All day Abduh would fast and study, spending the night in prayer and chanting and reading the Koran. He adopted the Sufi practice of asceticism, wearing a rough garment and going barefoot; he walked with his eyes downcast, speaking to no one. According to his own testimony, he at times lost all contact with reality and entered into trancelike states, moving in an imaginary world and conversing with the spirits of men long dead.

Under Afghani's tutelage Abduh gradually dropped some of his more eccentric qualities and began to develop into an advocate of the science of logic. Aside from the Sufi mystics, he began to absorb the works of Aristotle and British empiricists. He was especially fond of John Stuart Mill, whose essays became widely known among the early pan-Islamic movement's leaders.

After Afghani's forced departure, Mohammed Abduh was inexplicably named the chief editor of the *Journal Officiel*, the official, British-controlled publication of the Egyptian government. That such a post would have been given to a man like Abduh who was virtually unknown except for his connections to Afghani's "secret society"—the official charge on which Afghani was expelled—is a show of the trust that London had already placed in him.

Working under Mohammed. Abduh, as his assistant editor, was Saad Zaghlul, the man who after World War I would lead the Egyptian nationalist movement and the Wafd ("Delegation") Party!

In 1883, Abduh joined Afghani in Paris, traveling then to London where he spent time lecturing at Oxford and Cambridge and consulting with British officials on the crisis in Sudan. In Paris and London, Abduh was Afghani's right-hand man in organizing the Indissoluble Bond. It was Abduh's job to handle the contacts for the society among the Arabs, while Afghani concentrated on Turks, Persians, and Indians.

When the French suppressed the *Al-Urwah al-Wuthkah* journal, Afghani and Abduh split up, Afghani traveling to Russia—where he co-mingled with Russian anarchists, pan-Slavist organizers, Muslims of Russia, and others who would be useful to the British later in the famous "Parvus plan"—and Abduh to the Arab world. For several years, Abduh traveled under various disguises throughout the Arab world, concentrating on Tunis, Beirut, and Syria. At each stop, he would organize and indoctrinate a cell of the secret society in Afghani's pan-Islamic doctrines.

Abduh preached a simplistic doctrine, but to the insiders he would reveal much more of the nature of the antireligious tracts of the Scottish Rite and the "one world" unity-of-mankind propaganda. Those whom Abduh found to be particularly advanced he would arrange to meet an officer of British intelligence from London. By this means, Abduh explored the entire network of

Afghani's partisans, including Syrian and Lebanese Christians, Jews in Egypt and elsewhere, and representatives of many of the minority sects and ethnic groups of the area.

The public side of Abduh's mission was spent constantly preaching the Muslim fundamentalist doctrine. Abduh argued that the Muslim world, fragmented and in collapse, could not progress until it was once again united under a single caliphate. Abduh blamed the rulers of the various Muslim nations and also the establishment clergy—who, in most cases, were paid by the political leaders—for the tragedy that had befallen the Muslim world over the preceding centuries. His secret societies were dedicated to Islamic revolt.

The British secret behind this Islamic revolt is exposed in Abduh's preachings like the following: "The cure for those ills of the Muslim countries is not to be found in the multiplication of newspapers—for these have little influence; not in the introduction of schools modeled after those of Europe—for these can be used, together with the sciences they teach, to foster foreign influence; nor in European education and imitation of foreign customs—for imitation has succeeded only in quenching the spirit of the people and drawing down upon these countries the power of the foreigners they imitate. The only cure for these nations is to return to the rules of their religion."

In 1888, Mohammed Abduh returned to Egypt and there received a personal pardon for the crimes of sedition for which he had been expelled by Lord Cromer. From 1888 until his death in 1905, Abduh was one with the elites of Egypt's political scene, and could be seen regularly visiting the home and office of Lord Cromer

himself. From 1895 to 1905 he was the confidant of
Mustafa Pahsa Fahmi, Egypt's prime minister. In 1892,
he had been named to run the Administrative Committee for Al Azhar mosque and university. From that post
he reorganized the entire Muslim system in Egypt, and
because Al Azhar was recognized as the center of all
learning in Islam, throughout the Muslim world as well.
Finally, on June 3, 1899, Mohammed Abduh was named
Mufti of all Egypt.

The post gave Abduh enormous power: he was the
general consultant on justice for the whole country and
particularly for the state, in all matters pertaining to
Islam. Over the next six years, he would place into every
key position in Egyptian Muslim affairs members of Al-
Afghani's secret societies and devotees of *Al-Urwah al-
Wuthkah*, and he would work unceasingly to encourage
the growth of the clandestine movement that, some
twenty years after his death, would be formally consti-
tuted as "the Muslim Brotherhood."

There is a direct line from British tool Al-Afghani to the
Muslim Brotherhood of the Ayatollah Khomeini.

With the death of Afghani in 1897 and Abduh in
1905, the mantle of leadership for the pan-Islamic movement fell to Mohammed Rashid Rida. A Syrian who had
been educated in Tripoli, Rashid Rida had become one
of The Indissoluble Bond at a young age. Like the others
a confirmed Sufi, he was upgraded through Afghani's
freemason society through his reading of *Al-Urwah al-
Wuthkah*, which, he said later, was the greatest inspiration of his life with the exception of the *Ihya* of Al-

Ghazali. Rida never met Afghani, but in 1897 he went to Egypt to study with Mohammed Abduh.

A year later, he began publishing his own newspaper, *Al Manar*, in Cairo. Rida intended his journal to become the voice of the pan-Islamic movement, in the tradition of *Al-Urwah al-Wuthkah*, whose few copies were still in circulation some twenty years after the journal had ceased publication in Paris! Copies of *Al Manar (The Lighthouse)* that were sent to Turkey and Syria were not allowed through customs, however, because of its critical posture toward "Islamic reform."

Al Manar proposed the same plan as Lawrence of Arabia: the establishment of an Islamic Society under the caliphate, with its central branch at Mecca.

During its publication, *Al Manar* carefully followed the progress of the proto-Muslim Brotherhood. The Young Turk Revolution of 1908 was praised mightily by Rashid Rida and *Al Manar*, but the later Turkish revolution under Mustafa Kamal Ataturk in the 1920s crushed Rashid Rida's hopes. Rashid Rida railed against Ataturk's attitude as one of "pure unbelief and apostasy from Islam, of which there is no uncertainty." As the twentieth century wore on, Rashid Rida bitterly condemned the beginnings of Egyptian and Turkish nationalism, and we have already seen how the Iranian Shiite clergy—including the young Khomeini—made it impossible for Mohammed Reza Pahlavi to establish an Ataturk-modeled republic of Iran in the 1920s.

The very name of Ataturk struck terror into the hearts of London's fundamentalists in the Islamic world, especially in the patiently cultivated Sufi mystical cells of Turkey. Since the middle of the nineteenth century, the British had worked to develop an alliance between several leading Sufi orders in Turkey, such as the Beqtashi and the Naqshbandi, and the "pan-Islamic" Scottish Rite of Freemasons of Afghani and his followers. Together, this British subversive alliance formed the so-called Committee on Union and Progress and the "Young Turks." The Sufi cults had also managed to secure a tight grip over the Kurds in eastern Turkey, a troublesome ethnic minority that spilled over into Iraq and Iran. Many hundreds of thousands, even millions of Turks and Turkish Kurds had been enveloped in mysticism and superstition. This was the breeding ground of the so-called Whirling Dervishes, and it was the backwardness that Ataturk declared war upon.

After taking power, Ataturk proclaimed in 1925 that from that point on Turkey would be free from "sheikhs, dervishes, disciples, dede, seyyid, celebi, baba, emirs, bakib, halife, fortune tellers, magicians, witch doctors, writers of amulets for recovering lost property or the fulfillment of wishes, as well as the services, dues, and costumes pertaining to these titles and qualities.

"The aim of the revolution which we have been and are now accomplishing is to bring the people of the Turkish Republic into a state of society entirely modern and completely civilized in spirit and form. This is the central pillar of our Revolution, and it is necessary utterly to defeat those mentalities incapable of accepting this truth. Hitherto, there have been many of this mentality, rusting and deadening the mind of the nation. In any case, the superstitions dwelling in people's minds will be completely driven out, for as long as they are not expelled it will not be possible to bring the light of truth into men's minds.

"To seek help from the dead is a disgrace to a civilized community. What can the objects of the brotherhoods be other than to secure the well-being in worldly and moral life of those who follow them? I flatly refuse to believe that today, in the luminous presence of science, knowledge, and civilization in all of its aspects, there exist in the civilized community of Turkey men so primitive as to seek their material and moral well-being from the guidance of one or another sheikh. Gentlemen, you and the whole nation must know, and know well, that the Republic of Turkey cannot be the land of sheikhs, dervishes, disciples, and lay brothers. The straightest Truest Way [a pun on the Sufi use of the word "way"] is the way of civilization."

Ataturk enforced his policy with bullets. Lodges and fraternity houses of the brotherhoods and orders were closed down and their organizations dissolved. Their assets were confiscated by the state, and the military swiftly punished anyone attempting to revolt against the decrees.

The Muslim Brotherhood was Britain's answer to the Ataturk challenge.

The founder of the Muslim Brotherhood was born in Egypt in 1906. Like most of his predecessors in the British fundamentalist cult, he was indoctrinated in Sufi mysticism at an early age, and was soon caught up in the Afghani and Abduh network in Egypt. His name was Hasan al-Banna, and before his murder in 1949 he would succeed in building an organization feared throughout the Muslim world.

Banna's father, Sheikh Ahmad Abd al-Rahman al-

Banna al-Saati, was a moderately well-known author who had been educated at Al Azhar under Mohammed Abduh. Enrolled by his father in the Sufi schools, Banna passed through a succession of religious societies. At the age of twelve, the boy was the leader of an organization whose name was the Society for Moral Behavior. He then passed on to the Society for the Prevention of the Forbidden. Early in his life he became acquainted with the mystic circle of the Order of Hasafiyya Brothers, and for more than twenty years, he was a member of this secret society. By 1922, he was accepted as a full-fledged member of the Hasafiyya cult and proudly wore the cult's tasseled turban and white robe.

Banna's guiding star was Al-Ghazali, whose books he read and reread.

The talk of the societies to which Banna belonged revolved around the threat of nationalism in Egypt as represented by the liberal parties like the Wafd. They also looked with alarm on the developments in Turkey under Ataturk. The process of economic development in Egypt and other parts of the Muslim world had encouraged the growth of scientific learning and schools devoted to technical training. This the Sufis considered a grave threat to the "Islamic way of life." Everywhere that Banna's circle looked, they could see signs of the "apostasy and nihilism" of allegedly anti-Muslim currents, and "the weakening of the influence of religion." Banna decided to form various societies dedicated to the spread of fundamentalist Islam among the ordinary Egyptian. Based in Al Azhar and the Dar al-Ulam higher education center there, he organized "people's institutes" to counter the propaganda of the reformers.

But the impetus for the Muslim Brotherhood came directly from the Al-Manar Party of al-Afghani and Abduh. By the early twentieth century, the Al-Manar Party had come to dominate Egypt. Among its members were the leaders of the powerful Al Azhar mosque and university complex, in which the Abduh faction had staked its claim.

By the age of twenty-one, Banna had been introduced to the leadership of the Al-Manar. Often, beginning in the late 1920s, he would meet and talk for hours with Rashid Rida. Through the older man's influence, Banna was confirmed in his belief in opposition to "Western" influence in Egypt, to *franji* (foreign) traditions; he rejected the cultural trappings of the West in favor of "pure Islam."

In 1927, Banna helped to found the Young Men's Muslim Association. This organization was quickly superseded by the establishment, in 1929, of the Society of Muslim Brothers.

Banna set up the organization's headquarters in Ismailia, a port city controlled by the Anglo-French Suez Canal Company. The company—the leading representation of British imperialism in Egypt—financed the Brotherhood, helping Banna to build its first mosque, completed in 1930. By 1932, the Muslim Brotherhood of Hassan al-Banna, joined by his brother Abdel-Rahman al-Banna, could claim branches in Ismailia, Port Said, and Suez, and it was spreading fast to Cairo and Alexandria.

Over the next years, the Muslim Brotherhood quietly took root, producing various publications, including a newspaper.

By the late 1930s, the Brotherhood was strong enough to form its first paramilitary branch, the *kataib* ("battalions"). It began with the creation of a division called the "rovers." The "rovers" grew out of the youth section's athletic training program; soon they were a private army. Their organization followed closely the pattern of Mussolini's squadristi; indeed, the British, German, Nazi, and Italian fascist intelligence services were helping to create similar organizations in many Middle Eastern countries—the Kataib, or Falange, of Pierre Gemayel in Lebanon is one example.

In 1935, Banna made contact with the increasingly pro-Nazi and British-sponsored Mufti of Jerusalem, Haj Amin al-Husseini.

The Ikhwan also looked for and found support from the corrupt King Fuad and later, King Farouq, both obsequious stooges of London who sat on the Egyptian throne. It began to be funded with state monies. Like Egypt's other fascist party, Young Egypt, the Ikhwan of Hasan al-Banna celebrated the rule of the king—while it quietly prepared for a violent revolution.

With the outbreak of World War II, the Ikhwan began to forge the network that until this day has remained as London's Muslim Brotherhood. First, the Ikhwan established ties with the Azzam family, including Abdel-Rahman Azzam; Fuad Serageddine, the leader of the right-wing faction of Egypt's Wafd Party; current Egyptian president Anwar Sadat; and officers in the Egyptian army.

In 1941, the first documented case of cooperation between the Brotherhood and a leading British intelligence officer, J. Heyworth Dunne, at London's Cairo embassy was reported. It was just the beginning.

Beginning in 1942, the Ikhwan began to construct its widely feared Secret Apparatus, its private intelligence arm that fast became a terrorist, paramilitary arm of the Brotherhood. As the Ikhwan prepared for its terrorist phase, it organized the Brotherhood into secretive terrorist cells.

Within three years, the Secret Apparatus had begun to infiltrate and in some cases, take over other organizations. One of the organizations it infiltrated was the Communist Party of Egypt, setting the pattern for the Brotherhood-Communist collaboration that would follow throughout the Middle East. This blending of "left" and "right" is the classic stamp of the London Tavistock Institute and Sussex University. Americans recognize it today as the "Islamic Marxist" movement that put Khomeini in power.

As the war drew to an end, the Ikhwan launched its first terror assault. Its goal: to destroy the sections in the nationalist Wafd Party, in the Communist Party, the labor movement, army, and industry that, together, might have forged a coalition to oust the British from the Suez and Cairo.

After 1945, a quiet alliance was established in Egypt among the palace, the aristocracy, and the Muslim Brotherhood. Critical to this alliance—the cornerstone of the British presence in Egypt—was Anwar Sadat. After his release from prison in 1944, Sadat met with Hasan al-Banna, who asked Sadat to mediate a deal with King Farouq.

Sadat's contact in the palace then was Yusuf Rashad, the personal physician to Farouq and the director of the Royal Intelligence Service. Sadat and Rashad had been close friends for many years. "We grew to be more than friends," says Sadat of Rashad in his autobiography, *In Search of Identity.* "We became perpetual companions. . . . I still remember the day he gave me John Stuart Mill's *Totalitarianism, Liberty, and Representative Government,* which impressed me deeply."

So was Sadat recruited into the service of British intelligence.

Via Rashad, Sadat served as London's link between the king, increasingly paranoid about the British, and the Muslim Brotherhood of Hasan al-Banna.

Throughout the winter of 1946-47, the Brotherhood functioned as a political wrecker, assassinating leaders of all parties and especially trying to block the possibility of a Wafd-Communist alliance. The Wafd, though split by factions and corrupt, leveled deadly accusations at the covert alliance among the king, Prime Minister Sidqi, and Banna's Brotherhood. The party's press attacked the "fascist terror" of the Muslim Brotherhood, accusing the "phalanxes of Muslim Brothers" of thuggery. When the Wafd would establish a typical "minority government," the Brotherhood would then destabilize it with a few well-directed atrocities.

In one case, the Finance Minister Amin Uthman Pasha was assassinated in 1946 amid public charges that he was a "British agent"—charges made, surprisingly, in documents published by the Royal Institute of International Affairs. In this case, Anwar Sadat was arrested for the murder.

The Muslim Brotherhood terror climaxed in 1948. At that point, the Egyptian government began to crack down. At first, Banna piously denied that his organization had anything to do with terrorism, blaming it on uncontrollable elements of the movement. But in November 1948, Prime Minister Nugrashi issued an order dissolving and outlawing the Brotherhood. On December 28, Ikhwan delivered its answer: Nugrashi was murdered. Within two weeks, Banna went on the offensive; he repudiated his earlier disavowal of terrorism and called the Muslim Brothers to *jihad.*

The result was not what he expected; on February 12, 1949, Banna was assassinated.

Banna's death shook the Brotherhood—but not for long. In Egypt's prisons, where many of the Brothers spent much of the two years from 1949 to 1951, the Ikhwan had been kept secretly alive. Exiles planted the Brotherhood in Syria, Jordan, and Pakistan.

A large Egyptian landowner, Munir al-Dilla, took charge of the Brotherhood after Banna's murder. Dilla installed Hasan Ismail al-Hudaybi as the Supreme Guide, Hudaybi being a brother-in-law of the chief of the royal household.

In 1952, the Free Officers staged their coup d'état that ousted the king. The coup was the work of many foreign intelligence agencies—especially the British, French, and American—and the Muslim Brotherhood, which surrounded an essentially Egyptian nationalist core. General Neguib, the regime's front man, was close to the Ikhwan. But within a year tension developed between the Free Officers and the secret society. In February and April of 1953, Supreme Guide Hudaybi had a series of top-secret conspiratorial meetings with Trevor Evans of the British embassy in Cairo. Acting on his own authority, according to official Egyptian government documents released in 1954, Hudaybi secretly told the British that he would lobby to grant Great Britain permanent rights to occupy the Suez Canal base after the formal withdrawal of British troops stationed there. The secret meetings took place right in the middle of the explosive Anglo-American negotiations over Suez.

The Brotherhood had been caught red-handed. As the Nasser government moved toward a confrontation with the British, the Muslim Brotherhood was directed by London to wage war against the nationalist president. In that, the Ikhwan got help from Israeli intelligence.

In a scandal that had international repercussions, a team of Israeli saboteurs entered Egypt and set explosive devices off at several American and British offices, hoping thereby to trigger civil war in Egypt in which Nasser could be brought down. But the plan was leaked and exposed. Egypt's *Al Ahram* and other Egyptian press called the Muslim Brotherhood, now officially dissolved by the government, the tool of imperialists "and the Zionists."

The Brotherhood once again resorted to terror.

On October 26, 1954, as Nasser was addressing a huge crowd, an Ikhwan member fired six shots at the Egyptian president, who went unharmed. As the echoes of the shots faded away, Nasser told the crowd: "Oh ye people. Oh, ye free men. . . . Even if they kill me now, I have placed in you self-respect. Let them kill me now, for I have planted in this nation freedom, self-respect, and dignity. . . . Remember that, if anything should happen to me, the Revolution will go on, for each of you is a Gamal Abdul Nasser."

Mass arrests and executions of Muslim Brothers quickly followed. Throughout Egypt, the terrorists of the

Muslim Brotherhood were hunted down. Hundreds fled the country for Syria, Jordan, the Gulf, and Pakistan.

The movement had been crushed in Egypt; but now it had a home in every corner of the Islamic world.

7

Muslim Brotherhood III: Clear and Present Danger

The young Syrian cadet was puzzled. Why was he being summoned now to attend an assembly? He had just checked the schedule posted on the activities board of the Aleppo military college, and there was no assembly of cadets for that day. He was surprised because the Aleppo center was one of the premier military training units in Syria, with a long and proud tradition, and such spur-of-the-moment changes in schedule were quite unusual. In fact, the young cadet was slightly annoyed at having to break his regimen to traipse across the yard to the assembly hall.

As he left the building, he fell into step with some of his comrades. Strange, he thought to himself. Not everyone had been summoned to this assembly. Just a couple of hundred of the aspiring young military officers in his unit and several nearby.

In groups, smartly and efficiently, the cadets filed into the hall, gradually filling the seats and awaiting whatever was the reason for the call. Something still seemed not quite right to the young cadet, for the usual contingent of senior commanders was not already present at the front of the hall. By now, the hall was full of neatly dressed Syrian cadets, and no one else seemed to be on the way. Yet nothing was happening. Used to discipline, the Syrian cadets sat there without talking, though some of them shared the uneasiness.

Then, at the back of the hall, the doors were shut. The cadet heard them close—and, then, very strangely, heard the heavy bolt fall and the sound of chains. Now alarmed, the young cadet slowly stood up to see if he could discover what was going on. Too late. The sound of splintering wood and breaking glass confirmed his fears that something was gravely amiss, and he looked up to the row of windows along the side of the building just in time to see the grenade come hurling through the shards of glass. It was the last thing he would ever see: the explosion of the grenade sent shrapnel flying through the hall, one of the pieces ripping into the throat of the young cadet. All of a sudden, other windows broke and other grenades went off in rapid succession. With all exits bolted, there was no escape from the reign of death.

After the grenade assault, a team of armed men appeared at the windows, bearing automatic weapons. In a deadly crossfire, hundreds of rounds sprayed the unarmed cadets from every direction. The carnage lasted only minutes, but when it was over perhaps sixty Syrian men were dead and more than a hundred wounded.

Syrian President Hafez Assad was just about to make the final preparations for his momentous visit to Baghdad, Iraq, the next day, when he heard of the massacre in the military school at Aleppo. His intelligence officers reported that it appeared that the organization that was responsible for the deed was the *ikhwan al-muslimun*, the Muslim Brotherhood. Because of the importance of the visit he was about to make to Iraq, and because President Assad knew that the perpetrators of the deed had intended to prevent his going to Baghdad to end the long-standing Syria-Iraq feud, Assad ordered all news of the massacre suppressed.

But within weeks, the report did filter into the Arab press and, then, was confirmed by the Syrian authorities.

It was August 1979. The little-known Muslim Brotherhood had made itself known once again. Skeptics, who had earlier scoffed that the Muslim Brotherhood had vanished in Egypt twenty-five years earlier and who dismissed claims that the *ikhwan* were behind the revolution in Iran, began now to have second thoughts.

The events in Aleppo, Syria, made it clear that the existence of the Muslim Brotherhood in the Middle East is a danger of the most profound sort to every nation in the Middle East—and to world peace.

What is at stake with the rise again of the Muslim Brotherhood to a position of prominence is the existence of the nation-state in the Muslim world. The Muslim Brotherhood does not recognize the existence of separate states; it wants to abolish states and create a single Muslim empire again. It divides the world into two parts: the areas under Muslim rule, and areas ruled by "heathen," non-Muslim peoples. And it proclaims a permanent *jihad* to capture and conquer the non-Muslim world. It does not recognize existing borders and state boundaries. Iran's President Abolhassan Bani-Sadr, asked about the 1980 border conflict between Iran and secular Iraq, its neighbor, replied, "Between Muslim states there exist no borders."

A display of the ideology of the Muslim Brotherhood was provided at a May 1980 conference of the Muslim Student Association (MSA), the U.S. branch of the Muslim Brotherhood, in a speech by Mahmoud Rashdan, the MSA's general secretary.

"We know the story of Kemal Ataturk, the 'hero of modern Turkey,'" began Rashdan, referring to the Turkish republican leader. "And what is modern Turkey? From 1924 until now, more than fifty-six years, do we find Turkey more independent or more dependent? Do we find it weaker or stronger?

"There are many Ataturks today. There is an Ataturk in Libya. There is an Ataturk in Baghdad. There is an Ataturk in Syria. And until these Ataturks are removed and destroyed, conspiracies will continue. And they will be destroyed, *inshallah!*"

From the audience came shouts of "*Inshallah!*" and "*Allahu Akhbar!*"

Rashdan continued: "These Ataturks who speak our language and think in the Western mind do not belong to this Muslim land. The Ataturks of the twentieth century have made much more damage than the tyrants of the old days. As the Arabic poet says, in the old days there used to be one pharaoh, one tyrant, and there used to be one Moses who challenged that tyrant. Today we have a thousand pharaohs, and we don't have a single

Moses. But *inshallah* among you there will be thousands and thousands of Moses who will destroy these thousands of smaller, mini-pharaohs!"

Again, the audience chants: "*Allahu Akhbar!*"

"Look at Saddam Hussein, a butcher in Iraq, a butcher of Muslims. And with whom does he shake hands? The progressive government of Iraq shakes hands with the reactionary government of Saudi Arabia. Saddam Hussein was yesterday talking about the Saudi Arabians as being reactionaries, as being agents of the Americans, of the British, of everything. Suddenly they have become friends. Suddenly, they have a treaty, an agreement, a security agreement. Suddenly they are in the same camp.

"And add to that Hafez Assad, a butcher in Syria. Both these people butcher Muslims in their own countries, yet they go get donations and put on a label that they are a rejection front. And so they lull the Muslim masses into hibernation. They think everybody is sleeping. The Muslim masses are not sleeping—they are awake. The Muslim masses do not believe these slogans, and they know these conspiracies. You know them. And they know that the White House in Washington and the Red House in Moscow are behind them."

Declaring Palestine then to be "an Islamic cause," Rashdan declared: "I want to make it clear that to us Muslims, Palestine is part of our ideology. The conflict in Palestine is an ideological conflict where the masses of Muslims under the Islamic tenets have to be marshaled or mobilized. We support every action or every liberation movement which indeed seeks to liberate *all* of Palestine—Haifa and Jerusalem—not only to raise ambiguous slogans. . . . Kings used to be assassinated because they accepted the partition of 1947. Now they are made heroes because they accept the 1967 borders.

"So my brothers and sisters in Islam, let us define and let us know that Palestine is a Muslim land by the definition of the holy Koran. It is part of our faith. Its liberation is not up to our rulers, because they will not liberate it because they have surrendered it. We should stop seeking hope or insight from these present governments, with no exception. They are the cause of the disease—they cannot be the cure for the disease. May Allah make us true *mujaheddin*. May Allah liberate Palestine through the blood and through the *jihad* of true Muslims from all over the world."

The target of the Muslim Brotherhood is not Israel or the United States—but the governments of the Muslim world's nations. Rashdan's is not an atypical speech. It is even mild as an example of *ikhwani* rhetoric. In 1979 in an interview, another member of the Muslim Brotherhood gave his views of the movement's present position in the following way:

"The Brotherhood has taken over Iran and Pakistan. The revolution in Iran is our success. In Pakistan, the same. The Zia government there is our government. Bhutto stood for the intrusion of Western culture into Islam. He was everything that Pakistan was not. We killed him for that. And we will use his death as a warning to others.

"What you see going on now in Afghanistan is also our handiwork, the work of our brothers in the *Jamaat-i-Islami*. India is next: the Muslims in India are beginning to understand what must be done. The revolution is also going to occur in Saudi Arabia, Egypt, and sooner or later in Turkey. This is a global Islamic movement. It has been going on for centuries. We are the bearers of real Islamic humanism. We are at war."

No matter to what extent the Muslim Brothers are aware of it, the war they wage is a war on behalf of British strategic interests. British control of the Muslim Brotherhood has survived since the days that Banna's teacher Riad met daily with Lord Cromer in Egypt.

Since World War II, a new generation of British Arabists has emerged to take command of the Brotherhood. In this chapter, we will take a look at the British "old boys"—and "old Beys"—clique that has operational control of the Ikhwan. That control is used carefully and judiciously, when a particular Arab or Muslim regime runs afoul of British policy. In such cases, the semidormant Brotherhood is called into action on British command and used to carry out political terrorism, assassinations, and—as in Iran or Pakistan—even revolution.

Years ago, the old British intelligence Arab Bureau was moved from Cairo and relocated in London. Nothing was lost in the increased distance between the command center and its deployed troops. Today the modern "Arab Bureau" is the so-called Arab-British Center and the Council for the Advancement of Arab-British Understanding (CAABU), and its now defunct substation in Lebanon, the Shemlan Middle East Center for Arabic Studies (MECAS). Together with research departments in the oriental schools of Oxford, Cambridge, the University of London, Belgium's Jesuit Louvain University, the Jesuit McGill University in Toronto, and Princeton and Georgetown universities in the United States, London's CAABU and the old MECAS mafia direct the Muslim Brotherhood of today.

The Ikhwan's calls for *jihad* are formulated not in the clandestine cells of Middle East cities, but in the professorial offices of Western universities. The "Bernard Lewis plan," for example, is the code-name for a top-secret British strategy for the Middle East. Its author, Bernard Lewis, is an Oxford University specialist in Muslim affairs and the Middle East, currently at Princeton University in New Jersey. Though active in tactical plans on behalf of Anglo-American strategy—Dr. Lewis was an attendee of the 1979 Bilderberg meeting in Austria where "Muslim fundamentalism" was the leading topic—he is primarily a scholar, whose assignment is to profile the ideology and characteristics of the Muslim world. Based on his assessments, the British can then decide what type of intervention will be most effective in shaping Middle East affairs to British advantage.

Lewis's studies of Muslim history are scholarly endorsements of the Muslim Brotherhood, promoting the fraudulent view that Islam's nature is represented by the fanatics like Al-Ghazali, the eleventh-century mystic, and not by Islam's historically proven commitment to science and technological progress.

Lewis's plan calls for the balkanization and fragmentation of Brzezinski's "arc of crisis" along defined ethnic, tribal, and religious sectarian lines. It was, not surprisingly, worked out with the aid of Israeli intelligence.

According to Lewis, the British should encourage rebellions for national autonomy by the minorities such as the Lebanese Maronites, the Kurds, the Armenians, Druze, Baluchis, Azerbaijani Turks, Syrian Alawites, the Copts of Ethiopia, Sudanese mystical sects, Arabian tribes, and so forth. The goal is the break-up of the Middle East into a mosaic of competing ministates and the weakening of the sovereignty of existing republics and kingdoms.

What is the role of the pan-Islamic Muslim Brotherhood in all this?

The Brotherhood's pan-Islamic movement is, to the partisans of the smaller sects and minorities, a dangerous threat to their autonomous existence. The British then take the role of meditator, making deals with tribal and ethnic leaders to sponsor their rebellions against the Muslim Brotherhood.

Case in point: Iran. Almost as soon as the Khomeini dictatorship seized power, the British began making contacts with the tribal leaders of the Iranian nation who threatened to declare independence from Iran. Although most of these groups—because of their hatred of Khomeini—have joined in one way or another with the anti-Khomeini opposition in exile, there is still the danger that the success of the Khomeini revolution will spark a series of breakaway movements by Iran's Kurds, Azeris, Baluchis, and Arabs, among others. These independence movements, in turn, would represent dire threats to Turkey, Iraq, Pakistan, and other neighboring states.

The Bernard Lewis plan puts the heads of state of Muslim nations in a squeeze play between the Brotherhood and those nations' own national minorities.

From the professors, British policy is run through the Center for the Advancement of Arab-British Understanding and like benevolent associations. CAABU is no fringe lobby group; its financial support comes from the stalwarts of British Empire policy: Barclay's Bank, British Aircraft Corporation, the British Bank of the Mideast,

Lazard Brothers, Lloyd's International, Lonrho, National Westminster Bank, Rolls Royce, and Unilever.

From CAABU the word goes down to Britain's "Arab hands" trained at the Middle East Center for Arabic Studies (MECAS), in Shemlan, just south of Beirut.

Recently shut down, MECAS took over where Lawrence of Arabia left off. Established under the auspices of the Royal Institute of International Affairs in 1944, MECAS brought together Britain's "Arabists," Zionists, and Arabs who were pro-British. Former Israeli foreign minister Abba Eban was a founding member. Joining him were General Ilywyd Clayton, the military governor of Egypt during World War II who worked with the Muslim Brotherhood; Lord Killearn, the British ambassador to Cairo; his aide, Sir Walter Smart; Martin Charteris, director of British Secret Intelligence Services; Sir Harold Beeley, private secretary to Queen Elizabeth; and Albert Hourani, a Lebanese member of the Royal Institute.

MECAS has trained hundreds of British intelligence officials and agents in Arabic language, history, and culture. Among its past teachers and students we find the famous Sir John Bagot Glubb Pasha and his son Faris Glubb; George Kirk of the Royal Institute; A. H. Wilton, Britain's current ambassador to Saudi Arabia; triple agent Kim Philby; Sir Donald Maitland; and Colonel Bertran Thomas.

From MECAS the British spun out numerous organizations to "advance British-Arab understanding." There is CAABU itself, the Anglo-Arab Association; the Arab-British Charitable Trust; and the Labour Middle East Council.

The most important of MECAS's offspring was the

Arab-British Center, based in London. Among its leaders and directors are: Sir Harold Beeley, currently cochairman of the World Festival of Islam Trust with UAE ambassador Mohammed Tajir; Sir Richard Beaumont; Sir Charles Duke; Sir Geoffrey Furlonge; Colin Jackson, MP; Peter Mansfield, editor of *Petromarket*; John Reddaway; and Robert Swann, a British-Thai intelligence agent.

Thus, in 1955, when the Muslim Brotherhood relocated its headquarters from Cairo to London and Geneva, Switzerland, after Nasser had driven them out of Egypt, the Brotherhood was making more obvious a relationship that had existed since its beginnings.

In Geneva, the Egyptian Ikhwan leader Said Ramadhan set up the Institute for Islamic Studies. Back in Cairo, Ramadhan had been indicted for the conspiracy to murder Nasser and was accused of having ties to Israeli intelligence. This did not prevent him from setting up Brotherhood headquarters in Europe. Together with Salam Azzam he founded the Islamic Council of Europe, which directs the Ikhwan from Morocco to Pakistan and India, controlling hundreds of "religious" centers across Western Europe, and through them, thousands of fundamentalist students and Muslim clergy in both the Middle East and Europe.

The most recent Muslim Brotherhood coordinating organization is the Islam and the West (International), founded in 1977, headquartered in Geneva.

Islam and the West boasts two "non-Muslim" luminaries: Aurelio Peccei of the Club of Rome, whose policies are realized in Khomeini's destruction of the Iranian economy; and Lord Caradon (a.k.a. Hugh Foot),

Britain's Jerusalem expert and former British ambassador
to the United Nations.

One of the organization's funders is the Islamic
Solidarity Fund, a subproject of the World Muslim
Congress, but another—the International Federation of
Institutions of Advanced Studies—is far more presti-
gious. It numbers among its funders Aurelio Peccei; the
Netherlands' Prince Bernhard, head of the Bilderberg
group; and Atlantic Richfield president Robert O. An-
derson. Anderson is also the head of the Aspen Institute.

The secretary-general of Islam and the West, Dr.
Marcel Boisard, a vice-director of studies at the Geneva
School of Higher International Studies, noted in an
interview that the first preparatory meeting for Islam
and the West was in Cambridge in 1976, with follow-up
meetings in Venice in 1977, and Paris in 1978. According
to Boisard, the focus of discussion was the need for a
"convergence between Islam and the West" in the
context of the "need for a new international order." A
$10 million budget was allotted for projects on "special
studies on the impact of science and technology on the
cultural and social life of both sides"; "studies on the
Muslim conception of human rights"; and "restoration
of Islamic institutions and establishment of new Islamic
centers."

The Protestant church's liaison to Islam and the West
is Rev. John B. Taylor, a director of the Geneva-based
Ecumenical Council of Churches. In an interview in
December 1979, Taylor hailed the Khomeini revolution
in Iran as the beginnings of an "Islamic renaissance."
"Other nations will be touched by the Islamic revival,"
he predicted, naming Turkey, where "religious clergy

will take over"; Egypt; and Algeria, where "the Muslim Brotherhood is very important."

This Muslim Brotherhood command network in Europe is what Zbigniew Brzezinski means when he says "Islamic fundamentalism." This is the apparatus that is prepared to bring the Islamic nations into an alliance with NATO. Through Salam Azzam's Islamic Council of Europe, the first steps were taken to accomplish exactly that, via the Islamic Institute for Defense Technology.

The Institute was created in late 1978 by Azzam's Council, and today Azzam serves as president of its board of governors, while Muazzam Ali, head of the Islamic Press Union (an Islamic Council subsidiary), is secretary-general. The Institute's inaugural seminar was held in London February 5-9, 1979. In attendance were a wide range of military strategists and officers from both the Islamic world, in particular General Zia's Pakistan, and from the NATO countries, with a preponderant delegation from the United Kingdom. The organization's statutes commit the Institute to procurement of the most sophisticated weapons systems available.

To get a flavor for the sophistication with which the Institute plans to further the Muslim Brotherhood cause, while at the same time cooperating with NATO, consider the presentation at that conference by A. K. Brohi, former Pakistani Supreme Court president (who cleared the way for the execution of Zulfikar Ali Bhutto in 1979).

Brohi declared: "Muslim countries occupy a geostrategic situation on the globe which enhances their importance in terms of defense, since many are situated on some of the world's vital land and sea routes. . . . Muslim countries must aim at self-reliance in defense preparedness. This will serve as a deterrent against encroachment upon their territorial integrity and their Islamic way of life which they cherish so dearly. A concerted effort has to be made to revive the true Islamic spirit to enable the world of Islam to meet the ideological, economic, and military challenges of the present era.''

With American and British jet fighters and tanks, of course.

But if the Muslim Brotherhood is headquartered in Western Europe, it is naturally based primarily in the countries of the Mediterranean Arab world and into the Persian Gulf.

Recent investigations have shown that there exist several intermediary points for Muslim Brotherhood activities. One channel of Muslim Brotherhood orders is said to flow from Lebanon and Syria into Cyprus—long a nexus of British intelligence in the Middle East—and from there to the island nation of Malta, which is allegedly one of the chief bases for the Brotherhood in North Africa and Egypt.

Even with its Western European and British sponsors and funders, the Muslim Brotherhood would not be the political danger it is, if it were simply a collection of small, poorly organized terrorist bands in the Mideast. For any Muslim nation, fundamentalist student mobs, fanatical sects and cults, and extremist cells of medieval kooks would be nothing more than a routine police problem. The Muslim Brotherhood poses its threat on a far higher level.

In every Arab government, Turkey, and many Asian

nations, the Muslim Brotherhood enjoys the protection
of ministers, intelligence and security officials, military
officers, and others at the highest level of government.

Investigators who seek to track down leaders of the
Brotherhood find their investigations mysteriously halted
on orders "from the top." Security officials and law
enforcement agents pursuing Ikhwan terrorists are suddenly assassinated. Politicians hesitate before opening an
inquiry into the Ikhwan because of direct knowledge or
rumor that some Mr. Big does not want his toes stepped
on.

The Brotherhood is assisted greatly by simple corruption. The huge quantities of cash that flow into the
coffers of several Persian Gulf states have created a
stratum of venal officials. The current special envoy of
the Arab League to the United States, Dr. Clovis Mak-
soud, exemplifies the phenomenon.

And this is not the root of the problem yet. The *real*
Muslim Brotherhood is not the fanatical sheikh with his
equally fanatical following, nor is it even the top mullahs
and ayatollahs who lead entire movements of such
madmen; Khomeini, Qaddafi, General Zia are exqui-
sitely fashioned puppets.

The real Muslim Brothers are those whose hands are
never dirtied with the business of killing and burning.
They are the secretive bankers and financiers who stand
behind the curtain, the members of the old Arab,
Turkish, or Persian families whose geneology places
them in the oligarchical elite, with smooth business and
intelligence associations to the European black nobility
and, especially, to the British oligarchy.

And the Muslim Brotherhood is money. Together,
the Brotherhood probably controls several tens of billions

of dollars in immediate liquid assets, and controls billions more in day-to-day business operations in everything from oil trade and banking to drug-running, illegal arms merchandising, and gold and diamond smuggling. By allying with the Muslim Brotherhood, the Anglo-Americans are not merely buying into a terrorists-for-hire racket; they are partners in a powerful and worldwide financial empire that extends from numbered Swiss bank accounts to offshore financial havens in Dubai, Kuwait, and Hong Kong. Does Bert Lance need a few hundred million dollars to bail out his bank? Try the Muslim Brotherhood. Is a major London conglomerate seeking partners to invest a few billion in an African raw-materials extraction venture? Try the Muslim Brotherhood. Does an Anglo-American bloc of banking houses want to start a run on the French franc? Try the Muslim Brotherhood.

Since the murder of more than sixty Syrian cadets in Syria, and countless other murders of major and minor Syrian officials since then, not one arrest has been made of the Muslim Brotherhood terrorists who have claimed responsibility for the atrocities. The wave of violence against the government of President Hafez Assad has powerful friends in the government itself.

Two of these are extremely powerful: Colonel Rifaat Assad, the president's brother, who commands a special military brigade; and Deputy Prime Minister Mohammed Haider, Syria's economic czar.

The story behind these two sponsors of the Muslim Brotherhood is a prime example of how the Bernard Lewis plan works in the field. Both Rifaat Assad and

Haider are Alawites, a minority sect in Syria that dominates the present regime. Many of the recent assassinations were directed against the Alawite minority—ostensibly by the pro-Sunni (or orthodox) Muslim Brotherhood. How is this possible? Sources report that Haider and Assad are secretly encouraging the anti-Alawite assassinations in order to strengthen their case for Alawite separatism and to weaken the central government. Hence, Assad and Haider—who reportedly have ties to Romanian intelligence—work along with the Ikhwan.

Historically, as most Syrian politicians know, the Muslim Brotherhood has functioned in Syria and Lebanon as the battering ram against the influence of the French, and specifically Charles de Gaulle, in the region. In 1944, when the British began their final assault to run the French out of the area, the Youth of Mohammad suddenly sprang up as a branch of the then-powerful Egyptian Ikhwan. The British influence revolved around the triangle of the Syrian cities of Homs, Hama, and Aleppo.

According to the Syrian press, certain official circles in both Saudi Arabia and Jordan give logistical and military assistance to the Ikhwan's terrorists in Syria. There are reports of paramilitary training camps in Jordan, where Ikhwan brothers are trained. In at least one instance, Syria also charged that the Palestine Liberation Organization—which has its own ties with the Muslim Brotherhood—was, in Lebanon, responsible for training Ikhwan terrorists who then assassinated a top Syrian official.

But the Brotherhood is also supported by the PLO's fiercest enemies: the Christian Falangists, who give weapons and money to the Syrian Ikhwan.

The Shiite Al-Amal group in southern Lebanon also gives money and guns to the Syrian Ikhwan.

And it is through Lebanon that aid to the Syrian Ikhwan is funneled from Israeli intelligence.

In 1979, Egyptian president Anwar Sadat met the current head of the Muslim Brotherhood in his country, Sheikh Elmessari of *Al-Dawa* magazine, at a banquet, an event at which Sadat declared that he has nothing against the Ikhwan and that it should be considered a loyal, nationalistic force. The Brotherhood has come a long way since Abdul Nasser officially dissolved the organization.

Of course, Anwar Sadat is a "former" member of the organization, and the Ikhwan operates in Egypt today precisely as it did in the days of Sadat's work for it: as an arm of the secret police. It is generally believed that political control of the Ikhwan falls under the authority of Hassan al-Tuhami, Sadat's special adviser. Al-Tuhami is also a liaison with Israeli, British, and American intelligence. Last year Tuhami declared that Egypt might "mobilize 1 million Muslims for a march on Jerusalem."

Egypt's official Ikhwan sits atop a plethora of terrorist underground groups that are not officially tied to it— except for carrying out its orders. One is the Al Tafkir al-Hijra (Repentance and Retreat), which traces its lineage all the way back to Hasan al-Banna himself. The group was reported to be involved in the 1979 taking of the Grand Mosque—Islam's holiest building—in Mecca.

Then there is the Al Gamaa al-Islamiyya (The Islamic Group), which began at Banna's Al Azhar university. In the last several years, the Egyptian police have carried out several arrest sweeps against this group. In Assiout, police found thousands of automatic weapons—many of them Uzi submachine guns made in Israel. During the Islamic holy season of Ramadhan, the Islamic Group put on display its military might, prompting Paris's *Le Monde* to comment that the movement rivals the Egyptian army as an organized force.

The Muslim Brotherhood has gained control—almost officially—of the governments that neighbor Egypt, Sudan, and Libya.

Since the appointment to the Sudanese cabinet of Sheikh Turabi, Sudan has been in the hands of the Ikhwan. Under his influence, Sudan has turned away from the relationship it had been building with its neighbor Ethiopia, and is now giving assistance to the Eritrean Liberation Front, a manipulated guerrilla movement seeking independence from Ethiopia.

Sudan has the potential to become the breadbasket of all Africa with the rich soil of the Sud swamp in the south, but it has never managed to climb out of the backwardness it has suffered since the country became a slave ground in the Middle Ages. Now the country faces an upsurge of cult movements of dervishes and fanatical preachers in its remote areas. Many of these cults worship goddesses whose origin goes back to the pre-Islamic Isis and Osiris.

The Ikhwan operates in Libya through the Senussi Brotherhood. The Senussi Brotherhood's power has diminished little since the coming to power of Islamic fundamentalist Muammar Qaddafi. In July 1979, it was the Senussi Brotherhood that organized the Islamic Legion of Egyptian, Libyan, and Tunisian cadre to fight in Uganda in support of Idi Amin.

The Senussis are extemely secretive, and inquiring journalists are told firmly that it is no longer in existence, and indeed, that no one "has ever heard of it." But in July 1977, the Senussis made headlines. A Lebanese newspaper reported that Sadat was planning to strike a deal with the Senussi. The society is based at a spiritual center called Kufra in the middle of Libya's eastern desert, which for years has served as a military base. Many of the leading families in Cyrenaica are members of the Brotherhood.

Egypt and the Magreb have their own Khomeini: the blind imam, as he is called, Sheikh Kishk, who leads the Cairo mosque. For years, the blind imam has been attacking the "Westernization" of Egypt, and the corruption of political life. He has also attacked the Camp David treaty. Yet Anwar Sadat has never had this agitator arrested; he is regarded as the "most popular man throughout Egypt."

Under pressure from Kishk and his following, Egypt's parliament has now passed laws to Islamicize public life. Alcohol has been banned, along with gambling.

Kishk's influence also extends to Algeria and Tunisia. In January 1979, a strange thing happened in the Medea region of Algeria south of the capital of Algiers, near the village of Blida. A letter began circulating purporting to be the dreams of an imam in Mecca, announcing the imminent end of the world. The letter asked anyone who received it to make a copy and transmit it to another person.

By doing so, the letter stated, the copier would go to heaven when he died; otherwise, if he failed to copy the letter, he would be condemned. The letter's circulation caused a panic among the peasants of southern Algeria, according to the Algerian *El-Moudjahid*.

According to Algerian sources, the exact same letter circulated in the 1930s. The center of the operation was and is a network in Kasr el-Boukhari in the Medea region. The Algerian newspaper reports that "foreign teachers" are spreading such nonsense, working with certain people at the Algiers University and the Mosque of Chateauneul in Blida. Kishk's fundamentalists were telling peasants that to pray on land that is nationalized is a sin.

It was further revealed that circulating among the peasants in that area were thousands of cassette tapes of speeches by Kishk—the same tactic Khomeini used in Iran during his exile.

It is one thing for backward peasants to listen to the "holy" words of the blind imam. It is another thing for Egypt's educated. According to the latest estimates, upwards of 25 percent of the youth on the country's university campuses have been persuaded to campaign for Kishk's "Islamic reforms."

"The MSA has kept away from Saudi Arabia as much as it can, but I think that will change," the Iranian leader told the conference of the Muslim Student Association in the spring of 1980. He continued:

"In Saudi Arabia, we are working with the faction around Prince Abdullah and the King. Also the educated religious scholars are with us. Since the assassination of King Faisal, the new ruler, Crown Prince Fahd, has become more pro-West than any member of his family. The Egypt-Israel treaty widened the split between the two factions, which, of course, increases our leverage. Fahd had counted on working with the Egyptian army to prevent the Islamic movement in Iran from spilling over into Saudi Arabia, but now he cannot work with Egypt as he would like to. The Abdullah faction is sympathetic to the movement, and is using its petrodollars to finance movements elsewhere in the Islamic world. They are working with Zia in Pakistan. I would give Saudi Arabia ten years—maybe less."

The Brotherhood's plans for Saudi Arabia find echoes in the Anglo-American press. After the September 1980 OPEC meeting in Vienna, the *Washington Post* wrote: "Saudi Arabian power depends on there not being another Iran in the oil world. The troubles at Mecca [where the Muslim Brotherhood seized the Grand Mosque] showed that the next 'Iran' could even turn out to be Saudi Arabia itself."

Protected by one section of the ruling family around Prince Abdullah, the Muslim Brotherhood flourishes in Saudi Arabia. Abdullah is the country's number-three man and is the powerful commander of the National Guard.

The National Guard was formed out of the remnants of the Saudi Ikhwan, which was the paramilitary force behind the takeover of Arabia early in this century by King Abdel Aziz. To this day, the various tribes of the Saudi desert—while no longer wielding their previous influence, constitute a set of mafias and dissidents that orbit around the person of Abdullah.

But Abdullah is not alone at the top among the sponsors of the Brotherhood. The former head of Saudi intelligence, Kamal Adham, and the family of royal adviser Rashid Pharaon and Ghaith Pharaon, his businessman son, command the Ikhwan. And Prince Muhammad bin Faisal, formerly the Saudi minister of mineral resources and water, declared during a visit to New York in 1980 that Khomeini and the mullahs of Iran are bringing about an "Islamic renaissance" in Iran.

The Saudi backers of the Ikhwan are among the most powerful and monied men in the Islamic world. Prince Muhammad is at the center of a small empire of his own, consisting of the Union of Islamic Banks in Jidda, with branches in at least six other Muslim countries. He has sponsored, in conjunction with European aristocrats, talks on founding a new "Muslim World Order," based on the so-called Islamic dinar currency.

That the Muslim Brotherhood is a powerful force—with the growing capability to fulfill Zbigniew Brzezinski's prophecy of an "Arc of Crisis"—is clear. What is shocking is that the Muslim Brotherhood has such strong control over events in the United States—a non-Islamic country. That is the story we tell in the next chapter.

8

Ikhwan, U.S.A.

"I have a package for Mr. Tabatabai."

It is July 22, 1980, in a Maryland suburb of Washington, D.C. The postman looks up briefly at the man who had come to the door. The man hesitates, perhaps having an inkling that there is something not quite right about the postal delivery man at the front door. But he calls his friend: "He says you have to sign for the package yourself."

Ali Akbar Tabatabai starts walking toward the door. He is the president of the Iran Freedom Foundation, headquartered in Washington. Until two years ago, he was the information counselor at the Iranian embassy in Washington, a palatial building on Massachusetts Avenue, but with the revolution in Teheran he suddenly found himself out of a job.

Since then, he had set up the Foundation as a vehicle of opposition to Khomeini and, despite threats from sympathizers of the ayatollah, had established himself as almost the sole public spokesman against Khomeini; many other Iranians—republicans, monarchists, military men—supported him, but from a distance. They were too terrified to appear openly.

Two years ago, grim-faced Iranian students, wearing masks and chanting mindless slogans, had marched in the streets demanding "Death to the Shah!" On U.S. television news, they became a familiar sight. Now, it is the others who will march; on July 27, Tabatabai has announced, the Iran Freedom Foundation will sponsor a Washington rally of thousands of Iranians opposed to Khomeini. The tables have turned, and this time it will be former diplomats, army officers, professionals, and the middle class who will go into the streets.

At the door, the postman is becoming impatient. In his hand, hidden behind the package, he is holding a gun. As Tabatabai opens the door, the "postman" fires several shots into his chest and stomach, killing him almost instantly. Dropping his package, the killer sprints down the lawn and into his truck speeding away from the quiet Maryland neighborhood.

It is still morning. Within two hours, the assassin, David Belfield, a.k.a. Daoud Salahuddin, places a person-to-person telephone call to Geneva, Switzerland to Said Ramadhan of the Institute for Islamic Studies.

Later that afternoon, Belfield—undetected, and carrying several passports, possibly Libyan and Algerian—flies to New York under an assumed name. There, he changes planes and, adopting still another identity, slips past authorities and boards a plane bound for Switzerland.

But it is not over. On July 31, 1980, a group of Iranian exiles, some of whom took part in the July 27 anti-Khomeini rally in Washington, which occurred despite Tabatabai's murder, are meeting in the home of Kambiz Shahraies, leader of the Movement for the Independence of Iran (GAMA). In Washington, Shahraies had been interviewed on television concerning the death of Tabatabai, and he had denounced the Iranian secret service, Savama, as responsible.

Outside the house, a young Iranian student and friend of those inside is waiting in his automobile for the discussion to end. Suddenly, as he looks up, he notices what appears to be a black American man peering into the house through one of the windows. The intruder notices the man in the car and quickly runs away, disappearing down the street.

Then, within minutes, the same man is suddenly right outside the car, tapping on the window next to the seat where the driver is sitting. The student slowly gets out of the car—and the man fires five pistol shots at his belly. Only one connects, but the student is critically wounded. The would-be assassin flees.

In Washington, investigators are following up leads on the killing of Tabatabai. The most astonishing report, verified from many Iranian sources, is that General Hossein Fardoust, believed to be the coordinator of Savama for the Khomeini regime, was seen in Washington just before the murder took place.

Other evidence is piling up. David Belfield is found to be a member of a gang of thugs gathered around an

Iranian-American rug merchant named Bahram Nahidian. Belfield, who is black, has a history of personality disorders and is revealed to have gravitated into the underground of radical Black Muslim cult politics since the middle of the 1970s. Eventually he had found himself in the employ of Nahidian, who used him as a bodyguard.

Nahidian, who is a strong supporter of Khomeini, is reputed to be the Washington chief of operations for Savama, and during the revolution he cooperated intimately with the "revolutionary" Iranian Ambassador Ali Agha.

Bribing Belfield with money and then putting him up at his "Islamic House" on Wisconsin Avenue (Belfield's last known place of residence) Nahidian takes on the character of a classic terrorist "safehouse" controller. The rug merchant is also close to the Muslim Student Association Persian-Speaking Group, whose Washington branch was founded years ago by Ibrahim Yazdi.

But Nahidian is not arrested. He is not even picked up for questioning. When local police start to investigate Nahidian, the word comes down from "higher ups" to "lay off." The police later say that Nahidian's arrest was blocked on orders from Benjamin Civiletti's Justice Department and Zbigniew Brzezinski's National Security Council.

Within twenty-four hours of the assassination, representatives of the NSC, the CIA, and the Justice Department, and FBI meet in Civiletti's office where they decide to place a screen of "national security" over the Tabatabai case. No more is heard of the case.

But, as the Democratic Party National Convention is underway in early August, Kambiz Shahraies and the

GAMA organization issue a statement accusing the Carter administration of cooperating with Tabatabai's assassins.

"The Carter administration's continued commitment to a policy of alliance with Islamic fundamentalism has now resulted in conditions of catastrophic proportions," the GAMA charges. "Since the overthrow of the government of the late Shah and Prime Minister Shahpour Bakhtiar, U.S. NSC Chief Zbigniew Brzezinski's public proclamations of support for Islamic fundamentalism as a 'bulwark against communism' in the Middle East have not only resulted in the institution of a regime as barbaric as that of Pol Pot's Cambodian horror and the seizing of American citizens, but threatens the entire Middle East with regional war and instability with the potential for superpower confrontation. . . .

"Unless this alliance is immediately repudiated, Khomeini's assassins have a virtual license to kill their opponents here and abroad. We, the publicly announced targets of these assassins, urge you to repudiate the doctrine of an alliance with Islamic fundamentalism, which does not represent the true tradition of Islam. We urge you to support a crackdown on the Muslim Brotherhood."

GAMA's charges were backed up by the results of an *Executive Intelligence Review* investigation of the Tabatabai assassination and its implications. Among other sources, the *EIR* had gathered information from police and law enforcement officers and Iranian exiles. According to its information, the Carter administration had reached an agreement with the Khomeini regime to allow Khomeini's secret police to act within American territory against its opponents.

Not only that, but, the sources report, since coming into office in 1977, the Carter administration has been protecting a group called the Muslim Students Association, headquartered in Plainfield, Indiana, where it has a terrorist training center.

According to the *Washington Post* at the time, after the takeover of the American embassy in Teheran and seizure of the American hostages, the protected Bahram Nahidian was in daily telephone contact with the students holding the embassy.

He is also in daily contact with the leaders of the Muslim Student Association. The threat of Muslim terrorism in the United States begins with the doings of the Muslim Student Association. Within a few days of the takeover of the U.S. embassy in Teheran, at least 300 Iranian students were secretly filtered into the United States using phony visas produced with the visa stamp in the Teheran embassy building.

Many of these "students" were given shelter by Nahidian and Captain Setoudeh.

But Nahidian is only the point man for the operational side of the Muslim Student Association. The man who gives the orders is one Cyrus Hashemi, whose offices can be found at 9 West 57th Street in New York City. Along with his brother, Reza Hashemi, Hashemi is the president of the First Gulf Bank and Trust, Ltd., headquartered in the West Indies. Along with his brother Reza, Hashemi controls a network of businesses that includes International Intertrade, the Arabian Trading Co., ITC Ltd., and the First Arabian Bank.

According to Iranian sources, Hashemi is the chief organizer for Khomeini's Savama in the United States. It is his responsibility to supply funds to Savama fronts in the United States, via branches of his corporate entities in the Bahamas.

Hashemi is not bashful about his activities. In an interview earlier this year with the *Executive Intelligence Review*, he admitted that he conduited money from Iran and said that he is also closely associated with the Muslim Students Association.

Hashemi also confesses to being a close adviser of Iran's President Abolhassan Bani-Sadr and a friend of Ibrahim Yazdi. Hashemi provides Teheran with counter-intelligence on opposition groups in the United States. For this he has reportedly hired Captain Siamak Dayhimi, a former fleet commander with the Iranian navy, who is on leave from Khomeini's armed forces; his salary is paid from Iran. Captain Dayhimi shuttles back and forth from New York and Rome, where he talks "with certain Italian agencies," according to Hashemi, on supplying Iran with spare parts for its army.

But Dayhimi's chief task is to monitor the activities—especially those involving possible military matters—of Iranian exiles in the United States. That puts Hashemi in a position of up-to-minute intelligence on the work of Tabatabai and the Iran Freedom Foundation.

Yet, Hashemi's First Gulf and Trust is permitted to operate in the United States despite the fact that it is not registered with any state or federal agency. Nor was its permission rescinded when the Carter administration blocked all Iranian assets in November of last year.

The Carter administration has also kept a blind eye

to the activities of Hashemi's first lieutenant, Nahidian. Since at least January 1980, the federal agencies have known that Nahidian was the Savama's man on the scene, that he helped direct Islamic fundamentalist terror in the United States, and that he is a controller of the Muslim Students Association.

It is public knowledge, for example, that Nahidian brought $700,000 from Iran—laundered through his rug business—to pay for arms for his terror squads. Since November 4, 1979, federal agencies have known about his relationship to Tabatabi's killer, David Belfield.

Belfield and Nahidian's son were arrested together at a protest takeover of the Statue of Liberty, three days after the taking of the American embassy in Teheran.

Nahidian also had official relations with the Iranian ambassador to the United States. This is revealed in court documents obtained from Fairfax County, Virginia, relating to the March 1979 incorporation of "Research and Publications, Inc." Listed as a nonprofit publishing company based in Falls Church, Virginia, Research and Publications puts out a journal, entitled *Islamic Revolution,* dedicated to spreading the Khomeini doctrine.

The documents list the director of this corporation as Ali Agha—who at the time served as Iran's ambassador to the United States. On the board of directors was Kawbkab Siddique, a founding member of the Muslim Students Association. A second Fairfax County court document, dated June 5, 1979, recorded that the "registered office" of Research and Publications, Inc., was located at 2046 Kirby Road, McLean, Virginia.

The building is owned by Bahram Nahidian.

"At first we didn't care," said a spokesman for a group of Indiana citizens who were worried about the goings-on at a nearby farm in Plainfield, Indiana. "But then a reporter for the *Indianapolis News* told us that they were trying to establish a shooting range there. We made some phone calls to investigate, and we found that some of the people who set up the center had been involved in violence in Missouri."

But Concerned Citizens, as the group called itself, got nowhere in trying to force the Muslim Students Association to stop the paramilitary training of its members on its farm near Plainview. "We tried a federal suit to stop them," said a member of the group, "but everything we do tends to get squelched. Somebody, somewhere, at high levels of our government, doesn't want this exposed. They are stopping us."

The Muslim Students Association began in 1963. Since then it has built up a network that either claims or terrorizes every Iranian student in the United States, a business empire, and a paramilitary capability. The Association purchased its abandoned farm in 1976 at a price of $375,000. The North American Islamic Trust, the Association's business arm, reputedly launders tens of millions of dollars annually for the Brotherhood's use. The Association also operates such entities as the Islamic Book Service, the Salem Agricultural Company, and Sun Systems. At its Islamic Teaching Center in Indianapolis, it indoctrinates both Arab youth and black American prisoners in Islamic fundamentalism.

In 1963, the MSA was but a loose association of Arab students on the nation's campuses; by 1966, it had been taken over by operatives of the Muslim Brotherhood who used their MSA Persian-Speaking Group as their spring-board. Today the leaders of the Brotherhood's seizure of the MSA are found in the top ranks of the secular leadership of Khomeini's Iran: Ibrahim Yazdi, Mustafa Chamran, and Sadegh Ghotbzadeh.

"Their takeover of the MSA was very subtle, very deliberate," said one well-placed source. "They insin-uated themselves into the ranks of the leadership. Their mafia made several trips to the Middle East for money. First, they floated a company in Cincinnati, and Mo-hammed Shamma went to Saudi Arabia to get cash. He would discuss their intended political and 'cultural' activities, and then he would say something like, 'And, you know, we also have a private company.'"

Just how vast the accumulated power of the Brother-hood became in the United States under the cover of the Muslim Students Association is shown by the existence of a $2 million computer at the so-called Islamic Docu-mentation Center somewhere in the Indianapolis area. In 1976 and 1977 the Brotherhood conduited up to $3 million through the Association for the project, through the person of Youssef Nada, an Ikhwan operative based in Switzerland.

It is believed that the Documentation Center has interfaced with the International Documentation Center in Madrid, Spain, run by Archduke Otto von Hapsburg, which is the headquarters of the black international *Die Spinne* terror networks.

In September 1975, according to documents, Nada was present at a meeting in Toledo, Ohio, where he met with three MSA leaders, Jamal Barzinji, Mohammed Shamma, and Abu Saud. The minutes of the meeting to plan out the Documentation Center state: "Project to be completely secret. Middle Eastern governments would put Muslim Brothers in prison."

Another document reports: "It was agreed upon that the Center will start its work by collecting all available data concerning the Muslim Brotherhood Movement (M.B.) of Egypt. The M.B. is the leading movement in the Islamic world and the one which deserves immediate attention in view of the biased and mutilated information that has been published since 1952.

"It is of extreme importance to underline the fact that all the expenses—from the outset of the Center—must be met by a relatively fixed income emanating from some secured investment of available funds. . . . It is feared that [failure to do this] . . . would lead to dangerous consequences, as the information may be squandered and may land in the hands of antagonistic groups, who would misuse it and/or violently fall back on the source of the information."

Abu Saud, known as the "financial genius" of the Muslim Students Association, once described his job with the organization as "manipulating currency," that is, putting the finances of the MSA on the level of respectability. With its several front companies the MSA is a conduit of secret funds that go to illicit activities.

For example, Abu Saud is the treasurer of the Salam Agricultural Company, whose president is a close friend of Ibrahim Yazdi. Incorporated in 1975 in Humansville, Missouri, the firm is today located in Marshfield. Extensive evidence exists showing that Abu Saud has drafted letters in the names of others authorizing the transfer of funds out of the company's account and into personal accounts for use in Muslim Brotherhood special operations worldwide. Millions of dollars are transferred periodically through the MSA accounts, here and abroad, and through secret foundations and Swiss banks.

Abu Saud also had a hand in the MSA takeover of the Sun Systems Company, located in Eureka, Illinois, which deals with solar heating systems and components. At the time of the takeover, Sun Systems was in line for a $250,000 loan from the federal government.

Millions of dollars—most of it untraceable and untaxable—sloshes through the MSA's front accounts in such entities as the Islamic Book Service, in Plainfield, Indiana; the Square Deal Laundry in Springfield, Missouri; International Graphics Printing Service in Brentwood, Maryland; the Cultural Society in Indianapolis; and the MSA Islamic Services in Toronto, Canada.

Much of this money finds its way into secret accounts in Europe, especially in Switzerland. One key money laundering conduit is the Megal Watch SA, located at 5 Place de LaGare in Bienne, Switzerland. Documents from the company during one period show that M Mekki, the company's president, transferred more than $50,000 to Abu Saud, who turned the money over to his son-in-law, Dr. Ahmed Elkadi of the Muslim Students Association. Letters show that the money came from underground members of the Muslim Brotherhood in Saudi Arabia and Egypt.

But by far the most intriguing business venture of the Muslim Students Association is the proposal drafted by Abu Saud for the North American Islamic Trust, the MSA's financial arm, for the construction of an International Trade Center at 125th Street in Harlem.

The Carter administration is considering a grant of

$40 million—$20 million more than the budget estimated by Abu Saud—for the center's construction. It is not yet known whether this gift has any connection to the fact that Abu Saud was once a financial adviser to the Libyan government.

Attached to the plan is a letter from Harlem Congressman Charles Rangel to President Carter which states:

"As we discussed during our meeting on March 8th [1978], the concept of an International Trade Center in Harlem can form the catalyst for a new development in American international affairs. . . . I am convinced that the Center should be established in Harlem as a public facility, such as the one in New Orleans. . . .

"The International Trade Center will involve a broad range of participants from American international business firms. It is imperative these firms share your understanding of the implications of the program for American minorities and Third World nations. The project will also need the continued advice and counsel from the administration, and the direct participation of Ambassador Young and Secretaries Kreps and Vance. With support and assistance from you and your administration, I am sure the project can become a reality."

The International Trade Center, however, is not all that Representative Rangel makes it out to be: a vehicle to promote industry in Harlem. His model for the International Trade Center—the New Orleans International Trade Mart—was a shell company, a front for a corporation named Permindex (Permanent Industrial Expositions), which has been named as the key agency responsible in the assassination of John Kennedy, and which was kicked out of France for its repeated attempts to murder President Charles de Gaulle. On the board of Permindex is Prince Guitierez Spadafora, the sponsor of Billy Carter's Italian contact points to the Libyan government.

The president of the New Orleans International Trade Mart, Clay Shaw, was indicted by New Orleans District Attorney Jim Garrison for conspiracy in the murder of President Kennedy.

There are 50 trade centers around the world. The marts represent not only huge real estate boondoggles, but their computerized monitoring of global transportation is believed by some experts to form the nerve center for controlling the $200 billion of the annual narcotics trade.

All of this is enough to demand a congressional investigation into the Muslim Students Association's links to foreign agencies like the Muslim Brotherhood, and its activities in the United States. Yet, no such investigation has been opened. The reason? The Muslim Students Association, like the Ikhwan in the Arab world, has friends in high places in the United States. One of them is Senator Thomas Eagleton, the Democrat from Missouri, who has periodically stepped in to pull strings with the Department of Immigration and Naturalization to prevent MSA leaders from being deported. Abu Saud himself was a beneficiary of the senator's favors.

The most important protector of the Association, is, of course, the former U.S. attorney general, Ramsey Clark.

It is likely that Clark has never relinquished the title

of Special U.S. Envoy to Iran since Jimmy Carter dispatched him to Teheran in November 1979.

In the summer of 1980, after President Carter had been forced to break diplomatic ties with Iran and to forbid American citizens from visiting that country, former Attorney General Ramsey Clark went to Teheran again. While there, Clark consorted with Iranian leaders, including those directly responsible for the holding of American citizens hostage. When he returned to the United States, he was not arrested for violating the President's ban on travel, nor was he ever prosecuted.

Clark is the titular head of an organization in the United States that, in effect, stands above the MSA. Among Clark's cohorts are such men as Professor Richard Falk, Sean McBride of Amnesty International, Dr. Norman Forer, and others who represent the unofficial "liaison committee" between the Carter administration and the Iranian terrorists.

It was this network that Carter called upon when, in February 1980 on the eve of the New Hampshire primary election, he wanted it to appear that he was on the verge of gaining the release of the hostages. Carter reversed U.S. policy and agreed to the formation of a United Nations Commission to investigate Iran's grievances against the United States: "An appropriate commission with a carefully defined purpose would be a step toward resolution of the crisis."

The Iranians had long been demanding a tribunal to look into the alleged "crimes of the Shah" and the role of the United States in Iran. President Bani-Sadr and Foreign Minister Ghotbzadeh had said that under certain conditions the hostages might be set free, provided the

United States confessed its "guilt" in Iran. By agreeing
to the U.N. Commission, Carter thus invited the world
to witness the spectacle of Washington apologizing for
its foreign policy to a nation ruled by terrorists and
Muslim Brotherhood mullahs.

For the architects of the proposed tribunal, Carter's
U.N. Commission was merely the first step. The pro-
posed kangaroo court was to put on trial not only the
United States and the Shah, but the entire process of
Western industrial cooperation with the Third World.
Professor Richard Falk, Clark's chief associate at Am-
nesty International who supports Khomeini through his
U.S. People's Committee on Iran, named the crime as
industrial development.

"Ramsey Clark and I spoke to many people and
made the case that nuclear technology in an undevel-
oped country will have to involve police methods just by
the nature of the thing," said Falk.

Clark and Falk's principal collaborator is in Paris,
Nuri Albala. "I know that one of the Iranians' main
grievances that will be presented to the commission is
the sale by the U.S.A. of nuclear power plants. The
Iranians are saying that such a sale is monstrous,"
declared Albala.

During this period, Norman Forer, an unknown
professor who teaches social welfare at the University of
Kansas, was suddenly thrust into the spotlight.

In February, Forer—a former leader of Israel's Hag-
ganah militia—made a well-publicized trip to Iran with
a delegation of fifty Americans for what he called a
"dialogue of reconciliation" with the terrorists holding
the U.S. embassy. As it turned out, Forer was involved
with Iranian Khomeini sympathizers here. According to

his wife he had trained some of the student-terrorists who seized the embassy in November 1979. They were "his friends," she said.

Dr. Forer's involvement in terror went back to the mid-1970s when he was co-director of the American Committee for Iranian Rights, along with University of Kansas professor Don Brownstein. Forer had earlier been active in the civil rights movement, worked with the Justice Department in the "mediation" of riots and other problems. In 1977, Forer, Brown, and Nancy Hermeacha of Houston, Texas, went to Iran searching for a group of dissident Iranian writers who had allegedly disappeared, and whose case had become a cause célèbre of the Amnesty International.

After leaving Iran—no "writers" showed up—they went to Paris where they were put in contact with Abolhassan Bani-Sadr and Sadegh Ghotbzadeh. Both men were then leaders of the anti-Shah underground.

During the same period Ramsey Clark formed his Committee for Intellectual and Artistic Freedom in Iran, which helped the U.S. National Security Council build up contacts between the Anglo-Americans and the anti-Shah forces.

After establishing a working relationship with the Iranian underground, Forer made several tours of Western Europe along with representatives of Amnesty International and the International Association of Democratic Jurists. He established contact with both Ramsey Clark and Richard Falk, and terrorist networks in Europe including the Red Brigades and the Baader-Meinhof Gang. Back in the United States, he became an advisor to the Iranian Student Association and the Confederation of Iranian Students, both groups that agitated against the Shah. It was then that Forer taught the students who, a few years later, would seize the U.S. embassy.

Right after the taking of hostages, Forer—on the invitation of his students—returned to Iran again on December 5, 1979, when he met with the Revolutionary Council in Teheran. With Foreign Minister Ghotbzadeh, Forer organized a trip to Iran for Reverend William Sloane Coffin of Clergy and Laity Concerned, Reverend William Howard of the World Council of Churches, and Bishop Thomas Gumbleton of Detroit, all of whom have been supporters of the Iranian revolutionaries since 1977.

Then, on January 17, Forer, again at the request of the embassy terrorists, organized yet another trip to Iran, this time to include a delegation of fifty people. The delegation was chosen, at the Iranians' careful instruction, to include representatives of U.S. radical and extremist groups, among them the Detroit Action Coalition, the terrorist American Indian Movement (AIM), the Brown Berets, the antidraft movement, and various black radical groups. Many of these black U.S. organizations had earlier tried to visit the Middle East independently to make contact with the Palestine Liberation Organization after the August 1979 resignation of Andrew Young.

During this same time, Bahram Nahidian was also in Iran.

Yet, every step of the way, Forer's activities had the complete cooperation and endorsement of the State Department!

9

On
The Brink
Of a New Dark Age

"We know how to fast," ranted Ayatollah Khomeini in response to the possibility of a worldwide economic boycott in November 1979. "We will eat the wheat and the barley that we grow in our country. We will eat meat once a week. Eating meat is not such a good thing anyway. We are a nation of 35 million people and many of these people are looking forward to martyrdom. We will move with the 35 million. After they have all been martyred, then they can do what they want with Iran."

Khomeini's threat to turn Iran into a nation of "martyrs" took the insanity of the mass suicide of 900 members of the Jim Jones's Peoples Temple in a Guyana jungle and raised it to the magnitude of an entire nation. Only a few months after Khomeini had come to power, the world had been shocked by the awesome discovery that the Chinese-sponsored government of Pol Pot had murdered nearly half the population of Cambodia. Under the careful watch of thousands of Communist Chinese advisers, the regime of Pol Pot and Ieng Sary systematically tortured and killed more than 3 million men, women, and children among Cambodia's 7 million inhabitants in less than four years.

Numbed observers who entered Cambodia after the merciful overthrow of the Pol Pot butchers found mass graves, huge piles of bones, and concentration camps in the country first used for labor-intensive agriculture and then simply for mass murder.

Cambodia's capital city of Phnom Penh lay in near ruins, a total ghost town, with rusted cars lining the streets, grass growing in the streets, and animals roaming amid the ruins and rubble. The national library had been ransacked, all factories slashed to pieces, the bank bombed, and the nation's currency burned. So great was the Pol Pot regime's hatred of technology in any form that even kitchen utensils were destroyed.

The Khomeini regime now threatens to take the horror of Cambodia, a small nation depopulated by half by a forced march to the countryside, and bring it to Iran, a nation that had started on the road to becoming an industrial power. However, in Iran, genocide is to be enforced not with bayonets but with the paroxysms of religious frenzy that gripped the followers of Jim Jones.

This is no exaggeration. In an interview with the French daily *Le Monde* in December 1979, Iran President Abolhassan Bani-Sadr declared that the policy of his government is the systematic depopulation of Iran's cities. "Teheran is a monstrous, parasitical city, which absorbs by itself half the national consumption, and poses an abusive burden on the state budget," he said.

"We will depopulate it by creating in the provinces industrial and agricultural production units."

Bani-Sadr was asked if that meant that he favored the Cambodia solution for Iran. He answered: "Yes, but without the rifles. By faith and persuasion."

In the nearly two years of Khomeini's rule, the Cambodianization of Iran has begun. The rule of "faith and persuasion" is the rule of the 200,000 mullahs who now control every aspect of daily life in the country. In Cambodia, the Chinese and Khmer Rouge Guards enforced their genocide by telling their victims, "This must be done. Angkar says so." In Iran, the mullahs say it is written in the Koran, or Allah demands it, or the Imam. In Cambodia, the Angkar is faceless; in Iran, the face is that of Khomeini. The effect is the same: the brutal enforcement of a policy of mass degradation.

In Iran today, punishments for violations of the mullahs' laws are public, after sentencing by the Revolutionary Court. Women are publicly executed for alleged acts of adultery or prostitution. Convicted criminals are put to death in mass street corner executions to, as one mullah put it, "teach people a lesson." Minor crimes are dealt with by public floggings; in some cases, the transgressors are stoned to death.

A couple accused of violating so-called statutes of Islam against fornication were buried up to their shoulders in the sand and then assaulted from a distance by a gang of shouting mullahs hurling stones, first small ones to inflict painful and bloody wounds, and then larger ones to break bones, and eventually, crush their skulls.

Like the Big Brother of George Orwell's *1984*, the

mullahs are omnipresent. Iran's radio and television have now been transformed into what Iranians call "mullavision." No matter what the hour of the day, the television carries nothing but the visage of a bearded, turbaned mullah chanting some prayer or reading from the Koran. What passes for "news" in Iran is also read by mullah announcers. No entertainment—movies, nightclubs, and dance halls—is permitted. Alcoholic beverages have been banned, although opium is plentiful. Early in the revolution, Khomeini banned the playing of any and all music. Rock 'n' roll, along with the great classical music of Bach and Beethoven, were labeled the "product of evil Western satans."

In the summer of 1980 it was announced that Muslims do not need furniture. Within a week all furniture stores were closed, furniture factories shut down. Similar decrees have wiped out florists, perfume stores, many clothing stores, and other areas of consumer goods. When Khomeini ruled that Muslims were forbidden to eat meat that had been frozen, the importation of meat was suddenly halted, and Iranians now face food shortages.

Cumulatively the impact of these measures has drastically increased unemployment and inflation and forced a sharp drop in consumption of both essentials and "luxuries."

Ignorance is the backbone of the Khomeini regime. When the mullahs decided that the loyalty of the armed forces could not be taken for granted, they decided to station several mullahs on each military base to oversee operations. With no military background and totally ignorant of any science and technology, the mullahs nevertheless issued the orders to the commanders on the bases. In one case, when told that American space satellites were passing overhead, the mullahs at the base told the air force to take off and shoot them down.

As in Cambodia, the nation's cultural heritage is also being savaged. Bands of fanatic mullahs, believing that it is their mission to destroy any remnants of pre-Islamic civilization in Iran, are reported to be roaming through the countryside with sledge hammers. One by one, they are attacking the monuments of ancient cultures of Iran, smashing irreplaceable treasures of the past and ruining priceless archaeological sites that will now be lost forever.

Iran today is being ruled by people whose mentality is that of a medieval horde. The return of Iran to medieval barbarity is not only condoned but sponsored by the same people who brought Khomeini to power.

"Think about the Shah fantasizing about nuclear energy," Ramsey Clark told an interviewer contemptuously. "It was a fantasy because there was no national reality for nuclear energy in Iran, because it was economic planning based on a foreign model, and that was denounced by Bani-Sadr for over twenty years as an economist. I know Bani-Sadr very well. His book *Oil and Violence* lays these dilemmas out very competently."

Thomas Ricks of Georgetown University also describes Bani-Sadr's program in glowing terms. The Iranian president, says Ricks, will institute a National Volunteer Service on the Chinese model "to lead the march out of the cities. The regime is insisting that urban-born Iranians comprise the leadership of this movement."

Cambodia shows what such a policy means. Most of the 3 million Cambodians murdered by the Pol Pot regime were from Phnom Penh. The forced march of the city's 2 million inhabitants began two days after the Khmer Rouge entered. Out of those 2 million people only handfuls survived.

In Iran, this is to be done—"not with rifles, but with faith and persuasion"—in the name of Islam and an end to all forms of "Westernization." The sponsors of Bani-Sadr in the West justify this policy, because, they claim, it will end the crime of "ethnocide." That term, says Richard Falk of Princeton University and founder of the Committee for Artistic and Intellectual Freedom in Iran, means the deliberate eradication of traits of culture that allegedly comprise essential qualities of the Iranian people. In Falk's view, the industrialization of Iran is "ethnocide." Conversely, the horrible practice of self-flagellation during religious holidays by frenzied Shiite cultists deserves to be preserved as an "authentic" practice.

In reality, self-flagellation represents the self-degraded obsession that would lead a nation to become "martyrs." The concept of "ethnocide" is a hoax, a term coined to rationalize the destruction of a nation on behalf of other interests. For the British interests that brought Khomeini to power, Iran is to set the precedent for eradicating the idea that the underdeveloped nations will ever be brought out of their backward misery and into the modern industrial world.

"I saw one shut-down construction project after another, said a traveler to Iran in 1980. "They look like big carcasses looming over the horizon. Everyone is unemployed."

Until Khomeini took power, Iran was on its way to becoming perhaps the premier example of the process of industrialization in the underdeveloped world. The driving force of the country's industrialization was oil production under the National Iranian Oil Company.

In 1978, NIOC was probably the largest petroleum company in the world. In the year before the revolution, it produced over 6 million barrels of oil a day. Construction was underway to expand output to 7.2 million.

Curent Iranian oil exports are less than 500,000 barrels a day.

The Shah's economic advisers were also planning for the future—when the oil would run out. In 1978, thirty-two nuclear power plants were either under construction or on the drawing boards, most of them to come on line before 1990. France and West Germany held contracts to construct $30 billion worth of nuclear installations. In 1978 Iran was also talking with the United States about a $25 billion nuclear package, but the deal was never signed because of the Carter administration's opposition to Iranian access to nuclear energy technology. Iran had also begun to exploit what were thought to be enormous reserves of nuclear uranium fuel. Projects on nuclear fusion energy were the pride of Iran's scientists and engineers.

Steel was the centerpiece of Iran's transformation into an industrialized nation. The huge Soviet-built Aryamehr steelworks in Isfahan were the leading industrial locus in the country. In 1978, Aryamehr was already producing 1.9 million tons of steel annually, and it was slated to have an output of 8 million tons a year by 1985, making it one of the biggest steel plants in the world. The parent National Iranian Steel Company had also begun to construct several other facilities; some of its plants were using the most advanced high-technology gas-reduction equipment. By 1983—had the revolution not destroyed everything—new plants at Ahwaz, Bandar Abbas, Isfahan, and other sites would have given Iran a steel-producing capacity of over 15 million tons a year.

The steel sector was also the university of Iranian industry. The Isfahan plant was the center for training skilled and semiskilled workers, engineers, and managers for the entire nation. "Our income is not only from steel sales but also from intangible assets of training," said a chief of NISC before the revolution. "We have a big turnover in labor, and that is exactly the aim of the government—workers learn skills here and take them to where they are needed. In fact, we run a formal school, a training center for 7,000 students."

The Sar Cheshmeh Copper Mining Company had made Iran the sixth largest producer in the world, producing some 142,000 tons of copper annually in 1979, with over 400 million tons of copper reserves under the ground. An entire new city had been constructed at Sar Cheshmeh. It had a population of 25,000, complete with mine, smelting, and refining plants, and new plants for fabrication.

Tabriz, Iran's second city, was the site of the huge Tabriz Machine Tool Plant. This multibillion-dollar complex, constructed with French and West German input, annually produced 10,000 tons of drills, pumps, lathes, milling machines, compressors, and presses. Since 1966, Tabriz had become the center of the machine-tool industry, with a tractor factory, engine plants, truck and bus assembly plants, and other heavy industry. Thousands of Iranians flocked to Tabriz to join the growing industrial labor force. Like Isfahan, the city produced thousands of trained managers and workers for the smaller plants at its vocational school. An additional 10 percent of Iran's labor force was employed in the automobile industry, under the National Vehicle Manufacturing Company.

Within six months, Khomeini's revolution had completely reversed the work to pull Iran up out of the Middle Ages. Immediately, $52 billion worth of development contracts in a dozen different areas were canceled. This led to depression, as hundreds of other, smaller projects went down the tubes as well.

Among the canceled projects were several nuclear plants that had been in advanced stages of completion, worth at least $15 billion; the $1.1 billion Teheran airport; the $1.3 billion Teheran metro system; the $1.9 billion Sar Cheshmeh copper works, already 90 percent completed; the Bandar Abbas steel works, valued at $2.9 billion; an enormous $6 billion project for gas injection and secondary oil recovery in the Iranian oil fields in Khuzestan; a $3.3 billion Mitsui Japanese plant in Bandar Shahpur for petrochemicals; the second gas pipeline to the Soviet Union, named Igat-2, worth $3 billion; a billion-dollar telecommunications system; several entire railway systems; a new port at Bandar Abbas; oil refineries, shipbuilding plants, steel works, and electrification projects.

The heartbeat of the Iranian economy, the NIOC oil output, was shut down after May 1979, from the postrevolutionary peak of 4 million barrels a day to its present level of about 200,000 barrels a day in exports.

Now, lack of skilled labor and management as a result of continued purges of the NIOC by Khomeini's Revolutionary Guards has destroyed the company.

Before the revolution, NIOC had begun to install complex gas injection systems in the older wells to keep the pressure high enough to permit continued pumping. This procedure requires some of the most advanced technology in the oil industry, not to mention qualified technicians. After the revolution, wells with this technology were simply abandoned, and pressure in the wells had decreased to the point where they may now be worthless.

According to former experts in the Iranian oil industry, many of Iran's oil wells are now silting up for lack of maintenance, and new wells may have to be dug if production is ever resumed. The advanced Iran computer system that once regulated the NIOC operation has fallen into disrepair.

In industry, the Khomeini regime has managed to destroy nearly everything the previous regime had built. Industrial production is now estimated to be 15 percent of its prerevolutionary level, with the big productive sectors—steel, mining, small appliance manufacturing—at a standstill.

At the Alborz Industrial Park outside Qazvin, west of Teheran, only 14 of 125 factories are currently operating. Alborz was one of the most ambitious nonoil industrial development projects, with over $20 billion invested in more than 200 ventures in manufacturing.

In 1979, the Revolutionary Council proposed to convert the cooling towers of the two West German nuclear power stations in Busheir into wheat silos!

Conservative estimates place Iran's unemployment

rate at 4 million or more. In the cities, a visitor can see hundreds of able-bodied (and often educated) men on the streets—without work. Many of the nation's city-dwellers have turned to opium. This has occurred in part because the Islamic regime has banned alcohol, but farmers are also being encouraged to cultivate the poppy, which brings a high profit on both the foreign and domestic market. The *Washington Post* has reported that there are at least 2 million opium addicts in Iran—that is, half the unemployed—with a big increase since the revolution.

As one Iranian recently described the situation: "The remaining literate and sensible Iranians feel trapped. Their own expectations are dimming and they are left with no alternative but drugs. There was hardly any opium in the country before the revolution; now it is everywhere. It reminds me of what the British did in China in the last century. You look at that population; they just sit there and watch the country being de-stroyed, and they become politically passive. That is what is happening in Iran."

President Bani-Sadr reportedly favors the method used today in China to deal with the plague of opium addiction: the government would administer small daily doses of opium to the addicts much as methadone is distributed in the United States, legalizing the lucrative black market.

Perhaps most horrifying because of its implications for Iran's future is the purge of Iran's education system by the medieval mullahs. In June 1980, Mozaffar Par-towmah, an adviser to Bani-Sadr, speaking at the annual convention of the Muslim Student Association in Oxford, Ohio, pledged to eliminate from Iran's universities "all the infidels." "After that," he said, "we will move to clean out the high schools and elementary schools."

All Iranian universities have been shut down for an indefinite period until they can be purged of Western tendencies and made "more Islamic." Iran's Deputy Education Minister Mohammed Jawad Rajalayn says that the universities may remain closed for as long as two years; others say for as long as five years. Special *komitehs*, or "purge committees," have been formed in each university to boot out those students and professors who are not "Islamic" enough. Hundreds of professors at the flagship Teheran University have been driven out.

A new Islamic curriculum is being imposed on all the universities and schools to "safeguard Iran's young against deviation and decadence." The curriculum is specially designed to produce a new generation of Iranians thoroughly indoctrinated in an antiscience, antitechnology, fundamentalist world view. History textbooks are being rewritten to eliminate all references to the accomplishments of the Pahlavi dynasty and the Shah. Instead of studying literature and history, grade school children are taught to repeat mindlessly such chants as "Khomeini, Khomeini, you are light from God."

In June 1980, Khomeini appointed a seven-man committee to cleanse the country's educational system of of all "imperialist influences" left by the old government. "The continuation of this same tendency, which is an unfortunate catastrophe, is the objective of foreign-inspired influences," declared Khomeini. "The aim is a deadly blow against the Islamic Republic, and any negligence in the proper carrying out of our education reforms would be outright treason against Islam and our Islamic Republic."

For that, the penalty is death. Several Iranians, for example, were executed for not throwing away ashtrays in their government offices that carried symbols of the Shah's regime.

Opponents of the Khomeini dictatorship continue to be terrorized through the deployment of fanatical mobs. On university campuses in particular, anti-Khomeini forces have been brutally attacked by the *Hizbollahi* ("Party of God") militia, whose armed gangsters are led by Ayatollah Beheshti and Rafsanjani. Recruiting amid the slum dwellers, the *Hizbollahi* has become the elite shock troops for the larger, but less disciplined Revolutionary Guard *(pasdaran)*.

What's left of Iran's military is now totally in the hands of the Muslim Brotherhood. With its sophisticated technology, the armed forces were a training ground that produced engineers, scientists, and professionals, as well as rank and file soldiers, with a good grasp of modern technology. It was also the bastion of hatred of Khomeini. The new regime has adopted a merciless policy of annihilating the officer corps with executions and mass purges. Thousands of army officers have been sent to the firing squads or simply murdered in their offices, and many more are in jail or were forced to flee the country.

The destruction of the armed forces was carried out by a small clique that took control of the Savak in the days immediately following the revolution, including Ibrahim Yazdi, Abbas Laghouti, the Chamran brothers, General Gharabaghi, and General Fardoust. By constant reshuffles, purges, and changes in command, this team managed to wear down the armed forces to the point that its leadership is nonexistent, and the constant executions after discoveries of alleged "plots" have terrified other officers into remaining silent.

During 1979 and into 1980, Iran underwent a process of continued, accelerating descent into the depths of full control by the clergy and the Muslim Brotherhood. The first to be eliminated in a series of government shakeups were the old members of the National Front who, by refusing to support the Bakhtiar government in January 1979, thought they could make a deal with Khomeini. Leading the pack was Karim Sandjabi, the chairman of the National Front and the nominal heir of Prime Minister Mossadegh, who served briefly as Iran's foreign minister in 1979 until he was replaced by Ibrahim Yazdi.

Gradually, every liberal or democratic member of the cabinet of Prime Minister Mehdi Bazargan was unceremoniously dumped from office during 1979, until finally Bazargan himself quit in the wake of the November 1979 takeover of the U.S. embassy. In the same month, NIOC Chairman Hassan Nazih—who had struggled during 1979 to keep at least some oil flowing—was forced out of office and eventually into exile. Other members of the National Front, such as Darious Farouhar and Admiral Ahmad Madani, were also gradually eased from their posts and exiled.

To say that Iran is now in the hands of the mullahs is to say that it has reverted back to feudalism. Sons of the oligarchical big, land-owning families, the mullahs are now working to overturn the White Revolution of the Shah and restore their feudal fiefdoms back to Iran's land-owning families. That is the power base of the mullahs—combined with their power over the Iranian peasant.

What kind of mind does the mullah represent? To understand that one must first understand the mental processes of a primitive shepherd who spends a lifetime of habitual sodomic relations with his herd of goats. Then one must attempt to conceive what must be considered the "religious needs" of such a person. The mullah is the person who services these deviant needs.

The "religion" practiced by these mullahs is a set of rules for maintaining an orderly, organized system of mass perversity. That is what explains such rules put forward by the Ayatollah Khomeini as the following:

"During prayer, one must avoid bending one's head to the right or the left, toying with one's beard, looking at the writings of the Koran, or any other writings, or at the design of a ring. One must also avoid praying when one feels sleepy, when one feels an urge to urinate or defecate, or when one is wearing socks that are too tight."

"The urine and feces of any excrement-eating animal are impure. This is equally true of the urine and feces of any animal which has been sexually possessed by a human; and of the urine and feces of sheep which have been fed on sow's milk."

"It is preferable, for urinating or defecating, to squat down in an isolated place; it is also preferable to go into this place with the left foot first, and come out of it with the right foot first; it is recommended that one keep his head covered while evacuating, and have the weight of his body carried by the left foot."

"If a man becomes aroused by a woman other than

his wife, but then has intercourse with his own wife, it is preferable for him not to pray if he has sweated; but if he first has intercourse with his spouse and then with another woman, he may say his prayers even though he be in a sweat."

"Every part of the body of a non-Moslem individual is impure, even the hair on his head and his body hair, his nails, and all the secretions of his body."

The mullahs did not come to rule in Iran on the basis of their own power; they were placed in power by men more evil than they—who would use the depravity of backwardness for their own ends.

In September 1975, the Aspen Institute held a symposium in Persepolis, Iran. The public side of the transactions was published years later under the title of *Iran: Past, Present, and Future.* In the behind-the-scenes discussion, the plans for reversing the Shah's industrialization program and for turning Iran into a model dark ages regime were mapped out. It is a bitter twist of history that the Shah and his wife Empress Farah Diba witlessly provided huge amounts of funding to the Aspen project.

Attending the Persepolis symposium were at least a dozen members of the Club of Rome, including its chairman, Aurelio Peccei; Sol Linowitz of Coudert Brothers law firm; Jacques Freymond of the Institute of International Studies in Geneva; and Robert O. Anderson and Harlan Cleveland, both Aspen Institute officials and associates of the Club of Rome in the United States. Other luminaries were also on hand: Charles Yost, Catherine Bateson, Richard Gardner, Theo Sommer,

Daniel Yankelovitch, John Oakes of the *New York Times*, and the cream of Anglo-American intelligence specialists on Iran, such as James Bill, Marvin Zonis, Leonard Binder, Rouhollah Ramazani, and Charles Issawi.

The Aspen Institute session stressed a single theme: modernization and industry undermine the "spiritual, nonmaterial" values of ancient Iranian society, and these values must be preserved above all else. Ehsan Naraghi, a collaborator of Abolhassan Bani-Sadr, told the conference:

"Universities and research centers in the West have all based their studies of development upon a linear, Westernizing conception of progress. . . . Human sciences, founded on rational objectivity, are today suffering setbacks and defeats. Is it not important that, having exalted rationality to ensure human happiness, we should now be induced to invent a special discipline—psychoanalysis—to cure the ills arising from *an overrationally organized life that is deprived of its basic relationship with the nonrational?* . . . Why should cultures like ours, in which man is considered in all his aspects, be deprived of their substance by following a so-called rational course at the end of which lies the vast expanse of the nonrational?"

He continued: "The people have needs and aspirations that are not merely material. . . . The intrusion of machines into the traditional system may well jeopardize this creative life."

Naraghi's praise of the "nonrational" was followed by a similar outburst from Hormaz Farhat of Teheran University. "America has become more and more aware of her exaggerated reliance on material values," he told

Aspen's gathering. "Conscious movements have been made, during the past fifteen years, to refocus the aims of life to the spiritual. This consciousness has most prominently manifested itself in the attitude of young people toward life.

"Let us now focus our attention on what has been happening in Iran in terms of the point just raised. The country is going through an enormous social upheaval. . . . I believe that the current revolutionary state of the nation, when important far-reaching measures are effectively enacted, provides the right circumstances for a national resurgence in the direction of a moral uprising based on truth and justice."

Spoken three years before the rise of the Khomeini movement in 1978, these words were more than prophetic. They were the marching orders to the clique around Khomeini to charge the Shah with destroying the cultural values of Iran and its Shiite religion by developing industry and "materialist" values. From 1975 onward, the Aspen Institute developed closer and closer links to the Iranian ministry of education through well-placed agents like Manuchehr Ganji, who introduced both Marvin Zonis and the Aspen Institute itself to Iran. Catherine Bateson, of Damavand College in Teheran, was a critical participant in this strategy, sowing the seeds of "antimaterialist" rebellion among Iran's youth.

The word also went to Professor Ali Shariati to intensify his activity. More than anyone else, Shariati was the guiding light behind the Iranian students and intellectuals who brought about the Muslim Brotherhood revolution. Shariati's special ability was to be able to cast the mystical, antiscience Sufi doctrines into terms that might be accepted by modern young people not trained in religious law. Iran's youth could not be won over directly to Khomeini's version of Shiism, so it was necessary to create Ali Shariati, who disguised the Sufi doctrines in a radical, almost Marxist cloak. Shariati is the originator of so-called Islamic Marxism.

So radically antimaterialist was Shariati that he saw a willing acceptance of death as the only legitimate "escape" from the material world! "Do you not see how sweetly and peacefully a martyr dies?" he once wrote. "For those not fully accustomed to their everyday routine, death is an awesome tragedy, a horrendous cessation of all things; it is becoming lost in nothingness. But the one who intends to migrate from himself begins with death. How great are those men who have heeded this command and acted accordingly: 'Die before you die.'"

Shariati's father was Aqa Muhammad Taqi Shariati, who had been part of the British intelligence freemasonic movement and had started the Center for the Propagation of Islamic Truth in Mashad, Iran. Of his father, Shariati says, "He stayed in the city, and strove mightily to preserve himself with knowledge, love, and *jihad* in the midst of the swamp of urban life." The elder Shariati, he said, was "in the forefront of efforts to bring the modern-educated youth back to faith and Islam, delivering them from materialism, worship of the West, and hostility to religion."

It was the battle cry of the Khomeini revolution.

Traveling often between Paris and Teheran, Shariati built up a cult following among the youth of Iran. He introduced Iranian students to the works of Jean-Paul Sartre, Frantz Fanon, Albert Camus, Jacques Berque, and Louis Massignon, all writers of the anticapitalist existentialist swamp, all funded and guided by the same Club of Rome networks that gathered at Persepolis.

Fanon's book, *The Wretched of the Earth*, in which he argues for anarchy and revolution in the Third World directed against "the West" and violence for violence's sake, became Shariati's bible. "Come friends, let us abandon Europe," wrote Shariati. "Let us cease this nauseating, apish imitation of Europe. Let us leave behind this Europe that always speaks of humanity but destroys human beings wherever it finds them."

Through his writings and the publication of his Farsi journal, Shariati became something of a legend. In 1977, he was apparently murdered, and although his cult followers—like Ibrahim Yazdi—blamed the Shah for his death, it is more likely that he was killed by his backers in the Savak in order to create a martyr that would spark a movement around his figure. Were it not for Shariati, few students in Iran's universities would have followed the mad Khomeini.

As the Aspen Institute and Shariati began agitating against the Shah, in early 1977 the Club of Rome's Peccei, Jacques Freymond, and others began to focus the Muslim Brotherhood in Western Europe around a new, synthetic, zero-growth version of Islam. Called "Islam and the West," this project held its first planning sessions at Cambridge University in England. Under the guidance of Peccei, Lord Caradon, and Muslim Brotherhood leader Maarouf Dawalibi, "Islam and the West" assembled a policy outline on science and technology for the subversion of Islam. The outline was published in 1979, and backed by the International Federation of Institutes of Advanced Study, headed by Club of Rome member and NATO science adviser Alexander King.

Islam and the West declared: "We have to return to a more spiritual conception of life. . . . The first lesson of Islamic science is its insistence on the notion of a balanced equilibrium which would not destroy the ecological order of the environment, on which collective survival finally depends." This argument was used to attack "Western" science and technological progress in Europe and North America.

Peccei and the Club of Rome then moved into the Shah's court. At a November 1977 Lisbon conference sponsored by the Interreligious Peace Colloquium—an organization set up by Cyrus Vance and Sol Linowitz— Peccei conspired with several leading lights of the Muslim Brotherhood movement, particularly with the well-known Iranian "court philosopher" Seyyed Hossein Nasr of Teheran University, a personal friend of the Shah. Also in attendance at this event were Ismail Faruqi of Temple University in Philadelphia and Khurshid Ahmad, former head of the Islamic Foundation in Leicester, England, and now the minister of planning for Pakistan.

Professor Nasr has been instrumental, along with Dr. Manucher Ganji, in obtaining money from the Shah's wife, Farah Diba, and others for a Club of Rome economic modeling project for Iran. According to Iranian sources, Nasr prevailed upon Teheran University Chancellor Hushang Nahavandi, an adviser to the Shahbanou, to funnel millions of dollars to the French Jesuit-linked theorist Roger Garaudy, for his Institute for the Dialogue of Civilizations.

The money was designated in part for the Club of

Rome's Mesarovich-Pestel regional planning model for Iran, under the partial supervision of its French coordinator, Maurice Guernier. Thus, Guernier and Garaudy became de facto advisers on economic planning and "development strategy" to the Shah! One of the outlets they reportedly funded was the Institute for Mediterranean Research, set up in 1977 by Paul Veille, a radical Paris sociologist, and by Abolhassan Bani-Sadr.

And so, whether he knew it or not, the Shah himself was funding Bani-Sadr!

Garaudy is an important figure in British intelligence operations. He is highly influential in post-revolutionary Iran and among the ultraleft in Algeria, as well as being one of the closest mentors to Muammar Qaddafi in Libya. Garaudy is a former Communist Party theoretician converted to Roman Catholicism through the influence of Père Lebret, a Jesuit authority on maintaining African social structures based on tribal witchcraft.

In 1977, Garaudy formed two institutions, the International Institute for the Dialogue of Civilizations and the Université des Mutants in Senegal. In recent months, he has published a burst of articles in the French press describing nuclear energy as a "threat to the very existence of the planet" and castigating "capitalist growth" for "breaking the unity between man and nature." Garaudy also contributes to the journal *Mediterranean Peoples*, set up in 1977 as a control channel for British intelligence among "Third World radical" networks.

In June 1980, Garaudy attended the U.S.-Iran conference in Teheran arranged by Bani-Sadr, featuring former U.S. attorney general Ramsey Clark. Before leaving for Teheran with a European delegation of

Bertrand Russell followers, Garaudy published an impassioned review praising Bani-Sadr's latest book, *Which Revolution for Iran?* Bani-Sadr's analysis, Garaudy wrote, is "valuable for its main lines not only for the entire developing sector, but even for our country, if we do not want to be late for the coming mutation." According to Garaudy, Bani-Sadr correctly locates the Iranian revolution as a "revolt of the people" against the "Western model of growth," and against the belief that the "primary task of governments in our modern world is the one of economic development, of growth and consumption, of progress, of education."

"We must thank President Bani-Sadr," Garaudy concludes, "for having, through his beautiful book, cast a new light on the future we can anticipate if, through nuclear power, we take a route similar to the one Iran took through its oil: the route of technocratic despotism within, of dependence on foreign powers, and of the loss of our material wealth as well as our soul."

Garaudy's influence over Bani-Sadr was one of many influences upon Iran's president during his exile in France. Bani-Sadr himself is a product, neatly packaged, of the same individuals and institutions who created the environmentalist movements and the terrorist shock troops typified by Italy's Red Brigades.

Bani-Sadr's experience is not unique in this respect. Most of his colleagues presently in Teheran, and much of the advisory group to Khomeini, were trained, either like Bani-Sadr in France's sociology-anthropology nests, or in U.S.-based institutions promoting an "Aquarian rebellion" against industrial society, such as the Stanford-Berkeley complex in California or the Harvard-MIT complex in Massachusetts. In all these cases, the post-

Shah elite-to-be were indoctrinated in hatred of "Western" ways. The simple equation, the Shah equals the West, became their motivating belief structure.

A slightly earlier "elite" was also trained at the same institutions, the Pol Pot-Ieng Sary butchers of Cambodia, whose genocidal "cultural revolution" became the model for what Bani-Sadr and his associates would do in Iran. Cambodia's president under Pol Pot, Khieu Samphan, was trained in the same Sorbonne center that produced Bani-Sadr!

Bani-Sadr's closest mentors and associates came from four overlapping institutions: the sociology-anthropology division of the Centre Nationale des Recherches Scientifiques (CNRS), "Division Six" of the École Pratique des Hautes Études (EPHE-6), and the National Institute for Agronomical Research. Of these, the most important is EPHE-6, which trained Bani-Sadr's thesis adviser, Professor George Balandier, a student of African tribal customs. EPHE-6 is the base for the ecology-antinuclear movement in France. While studying "agrarian reform" Maoism under Balandier, Bani-Sadr was influenced directly or indirectly by the following individuals:

—Paul Veille, "Marxist sociologist," CNRS, Institute for Mediterranean Research.

—Réné Dumont, a radical agronomist at the CNRS, who is honorary president of the Friends of the Earth, and a founder of Ecoropa, the European environmentalist umbrella organization. Dumont, a World Bank adviser, has been expelled from both Cuba and Algeria for being a CIA agent. In 1976, Dumont led an expedition to Iran to investigate the agricultural system there, and has since become an adviser to Khomeini.

—Michel Crozier, an EPHE-6 theorist from Tavistock Institute at Britain's Sussex University, who helped to coordinate the 1968 destabilization of the Charles de Gaulle government.

—Jean-Pierre Vigier, a radical scientist at CNRS who ran the 1968 secretive "Command Center of the Revolution" against de Gaulle.

Other individuals who worked with Bani-Sadr, and all of whom participated in the British and Israeli intelligence destabilization of de Gaulle and France during the 1960s and 1970s, include Michel Foucault, Jacques Soustelle, Charles Bettelheim, Claude Levi-Strauss, and the late Henri Corbin.

It is these gentlemen, backed by the Bertrand Russell Peace Foundation, the Lelio Basso Foundation, the Transnational Institute, and the Ramsey Clarks and Richard Falks of the New York Council on Foreign Relations, whom we have to thank for the current horror in Iran called—by Bani-Sadr—"Cambodianization by persuasion."

10

The
Soviet Factor:
'Kim' Philby

The more sinister, hidden features of the Khomeini revolution begin to emerge when one considers how many powerful intelligence services collaborated to elevate him first to a position of preeminence, and then to power. The Intelligence Service of Great Britain played the principal coordinating role drawing on the resources of American intelligence, Israeli intelligence—and also Soviet intelligence.

Ultimately, a full investigation of the behind-the-scenes intrigues which led to the emergence of Khomeini, will finally shed light upon the most controversial and still unresolved 20th century spy mystery: the legend of "The Third Man," General Harold Adrian Russell "Kim" Philby of the KGB, the Soviet Committee on State Security.

"Kim" Philby, one of the most senior chiefs of British intelligence, during the Second World War was in charge of training American intelligence officers for the American Office of Strategic Services, which later became the CIA. Among his pupils was James Jesus Angleton, who headed the CIA's Counterintelligence Section until his ouster in 1973.

According to the official legend of the intelligence services, two suspected Soviet spies within the British intelligence establishment, Burgess and Maclean, staged a spectacular defection into the Soviet Union before the ongoing official British investigation against them could catch its targets. This occurred in 1951, and for five years, the world was awash with speculation as to the identity of the "Third Man" who tipped off Burgess and Maclean and thus made their defection possible.

In 1955, "Kim" Philby was officially identified as the "Third Man,"—and then forgiven his trespass and reassigned to a semi-official intelligence capacity in the Middle East. During the period 1955 to 1963, "Kim" Philby was handed Britain's Middle East networks and assets by his father, St. John Philby, the most accomplished Arabist intelligence operative in the history of the British Empire. When this transfer of power from father to son was completed, "Kim" Philby moved into the Soviet Union under cover of "defection."

For many years, Moscow kept Philby in mothballs. He resurfaced into public prominence at exactly the same time as the Khomeini revolution was shifted to high gear by London. In 1978, after many years of official silence, Philby was appointed policy coordinator for Syria, Iraq, Jordan, and the Arabian Peninsula at the Soviet Foreign Ministry. The next year, 1979, as Khomeini took power in Teheran, Philby was promoted to the rank of General of the KGB. Then in 1980, the unprecedented occurred: Kim Philby, the master spy, granted a unique interview to *Izvestia*, to signal that he enjoyed the full confidence of the Soviet government. That interview was published shortly *after* the Queen's Art Curator, Sir Anthony Blunt, was revealed to have been Kim Philby's intelligence controller for Britain's Royal Court.

Sources inside intelligence services have reported that the "religious fundamentalist" revolutions plotted for the 1980s were the brainchild of a small team of strategists including Queen Elizabeth II; her personal theological adviser Herbert Waddams, chief of the Foreign Missions Section of the Anglican Church and the real power in the World Council of Churches; and the old chiefs of the "Canadian" SOE, including the old elite team of the "Cambridge Apostles"—Burgess, Maclean, Philby and Anthony Blunt—now maintaining intelligence networks in the East Bloc. When some powerful insiders within England tried to oppose this insanity of sacerdotal revolutions, exceptional things occurred. Lord Mountbatten was assassinated; the Archbishop of Canterbury died prematurely, to be replaced by a man devoted to the cause of "liberation theology" and sacerdotal revolutions generally. A program of rapprochement between the Anglican Church and the Jesuit "liberation theology" wing of Roman Catholicism was worked out and announced, including a proviso in British law which will for the first time allow Great Britain's Crown Prince to marry a Roman Catholic.

Apparently, opponents of this strategy in England resorted to the ploy of exposing Sir Anthony Blunt as Philby's controller, thus destroying the myth of Philby being a long-term dedicated communist who had penetrated British intelligence on behalf of the Soviet Union.

"Kim" Philby was now exposed as a "triple" agent, a British intelligence operative disguised as a "Soviet double-agent."

Under ordinary circumstances, on the basis of the Anthony Blunt revelations, the Soviet authorities would have enough evidence to have Philby taken out and shot. It did not happen. Instead, the Soviet government signaled its confidence in Philby by publishing that unprecedented *Izvestia* interview. What transpired we shall probably never find out in detail. In general outline, however, it is evident that a deal of sorts was struck between the British and Soviet services, involving a shared agreement to have Iran destabilized, the Shah overthrown, Ayatollah Khomeini installed to power and United States influence removed from Iran. The British would gain a major strategic bridgehead for the further launching of their worldwide "sacerdotal revolution"; the Soviets, unimpressed by the power of religious ideas, would use the mullahs to dismantle American military power in the Gulf.

Thus, a cynical arrangement was clinched between the purely military-oriented Soviet High Command and the more sophisticated British gamemasters whose insight into the uses of the "religious fundamentalist weapon" is not shared by the crude Soviets. Brzezinski, for instance, is confident that Islamic fundamentalism will ultimately undermine and destabilize Soviet cohesion in Central Asia. Brzezinski's Soviet rivals, on the other hand, are confident that Islamic fundamentalism will tear apart American military power in the Middle East. The British, as the go-between, arranged that both the American NSC and the Soviets would place their bets in favor of Khomeini and against the Shah.

Thus, the astounding spectacle emerged of four of the most legendary intelligence services in the world, all bitter rivals, collaborating to support Khomeini: KBG, CIA, Israeli Mossad, and British SIS.

The man upon whose personality and reputation this deal of convenience was clinched is "Kim" Philby, the SIS gamemaster who betrayed CIA secrets to the KGB, the teacher and friend of the Mossad's Teddy Kolek, and the teacher and *amour propre* of the chief of the CIA's Israel Desk, James Angleton. Hence the reemergence of Kim Philby into public life at the same time as the meteoric rise of Ayatollah Khomeini.

Key to understanding General "Kim" Philby of the KGB is his father, Harry St.-John Bridger Philby, Great Britain's chief strategist for the Muslim world for forty years, and the brain guiding the "Arab Bureau" of British intelligence throughout his life. The last five years of St.-John Philby's life were spent in transferring his knowledge, connections, and networks to his son "Kim." Together, Philby *pere et fils* inhabit the nether world where Anglo-Jesuit long-term strategic intelligence meets and meshes with the radical Marxist "Bukharinite" faction of the Soviet KGB.

St.-John Philby, the father, grew up at the turn of the century in the rarified intellectual centers of Cambridge, where waning Victorian England was still celebrating what it called the "Three Miracles of the 19th Century." These were three potent creations of British intelligence, three major ideological projects designed for use in running the Empire: 1) liberalism as an international political tendency; 2) orientalist studies as shaped by Sir Richard Burton and Lord Acton, Queen Victoria's specialist on religious-ideological warfare; and

3) Marxism as a systematic "belief structure" for managing Jacobin movements against governments and powers rivaling the Empire.

During the time of St.-John's youth, the scholarly chiefs of British intelligence were quite open, within their small circle, in bragging about these achievements.

Following the profile of many of Britain's leading secret intelligence specialists, St.-John Philby was recruited out of an upper middle class English family and brought to Cambridge University in 1904. At Cambridge, Philby was introduced into the circles of the top British Roundtable intelligence personnel, and gravitated into the ranks of the newly established "Cambridge Fabians." The Fabians, precursors of the Fabian Society, were spawned at Cambridge as part of the Roundtable's overall efforts to synthesize a seeming "left-wing" apparatus of the British SIS. Later, after leaving Cambridge, in the 1920s Philby would become a member of the Fabian Society of Great Britain.

Revealing his early commitment to the value of cults and "religious" feeling as a mechanism of social control—an insight that he would later use in contributing to the establishment of the Muslim Brotherhood in the Arab world—Philby concentrated his undergraduate research and theses on religion. In one of his youthful papers, he wrote that religion is "of all conventions the greatest—so universal, so fundamental a part of the human system, so strong in its resistance to all opposition." In another, signal work, Philby compared the influence of the philosopher Aristotle to that of religious fundamentalists, and he concluded that religion is indeed "far more effective."

This tendency of the young St.-John Philby to emphasize the sacerdotal in political intelligence operations was later developed into the central operating doctrine of the Secret Intelligence Service by its renowned chief, the historian Arnold Joseph Toynbee. During the First World War and the Versailles Treaty period, Toynbee served as head of British intelligence in the Balkans and the Middle East and during World War II, he was chief of the combined intelligence services for Winston Churchill.

Arnold Toynbee of Oxford, St.-John's direct superior in the intelligence service, was one of the most prominent popularizers of the doctrine that "in the long sweep of history," religious ideology, sacerdotal authority, and the religious sense of identity of the individual are historical forces far superior to currently prevailing forms of national identity and national authority. Hence, Toynbee repeatedly argued, if one is to ultimately construct and control a lasting, stable imperial world order in the "final analysis," and in the "long sweep of history," one must engineer the intelligence and subversion networks which will be capable of imposing a sacerdotal authority and a religious sense of identity upon populations that are currently ruled by secular authorities and national senses of identity.

In his final year at Cambridge in 1907, Philby was ushered into the innermost elite of the epistemological warriors of British intelligence. The "guardian and guide" for his graduate year was none other than E. G. Browne, the successor of Sir Richard Burton, the architect of the 1905 Persian "revolution," and the number-one expert for the British Roundtable on Islamic mysticism, Persia, and Sufism. Together with Wilfrid S. Blunt, Browne had been the chief sponsor of the granddaddy of the soon-to-be Muslim Brotherhood, the Scottish Rite freemasonic cultist and pan-Islamic organizer, Jamaleddine al-Afghani. Working intensively with Browne during 1907, Philby learned the secrets of Britain's strategic use of synthetic, radical nationalist, and religious cults. Philby also polished up his Persian and Hindustani, and started to learn Urdu. During his career he became fluent in these languages, as well as Arabic, Turkish, and several local dialects.

As World War I approached, the young St.-John was sent to India as a junior political intelligence officer in the India Office. The years in India served as his training period; he became involved during those years in projects to heighten Hindu-Muslim tensions in India, which later created the basis for dividing the Indian Subcontinent into two religiously based entities, India and Pakistan. Although he assimilated the "divide and conquer" strategy of British rule in India, his years with the master E. G. Browne also taught him the value of encouraging nationalist movements—even nationalist movements primarily dedicated to removing British rule—as a means of finally perpetuating British influence.

The years of the World War saw the implementation of this strategy in its quintessential form by the new Arab Bureau of the British SIS in Cairo, established under D. G. Hogarth of Oxford University's Ashmolean Museum. The best-known operative of the Arab Bureau in the period was the famous T. E. Lawrence "of Arabia," who was busily at work in the Hijaz region of the western Arabian Peninsula with Sharif Hussein of Mecca in "the Arab Revolt." That strategy involved the transfer of large quantities of British gold to the Arab tribal armies of the Hijaz, in order to encourage an Arab independence movement aimed at the disintegration of the Ottoman Empire.

In 1915, Philby was assigned to Mesopotamia (Iraq), then under occupation by British and Indian troops, and under the command of the India Office. Strategically, a conflict in policy had begun to develop between the India Office and the Arab Bureau. Guided by Hogarth, Gertrude Bell, and Lawrence, the Arab Bureau was encouraging the growth of British-controlled Muslim fundamentalism and Arab nationalism, while the somewhat more conservative government of India and certain factions of the British India Office were a bit more reluctant to spark off a Muslim rebellion, fearing that it could spread unchecked into India from the Arab world and touch off a revolt against British rule there. For his part, in Iraq, Philby gradually gravitated to the view of the Arab Bureau. He was helped along by the guidance of Gertrude Bell, a hardy female traveler for the British SIS who was one of the leading lights of London's policy toward the Arab world. For years afterward, Bell and Philby would be confidantes.

From 1918 until his death more than forty years later, St.-John Philby was the chief of operations for British intelligence in Saudi Arabia.

At the beginning, Philby delved into the mysteries of tribal politics in the Arabian Peninsula. Soon after his assignment to the Arab world, Philby had familiarized himself with every nook and cranny in Arabia, and by the time of his death he became known as the premier trailblazer in its desert sands. His tombstone reads: "Greatest of the Arabian Explorers."

In his first years in Arabia, he carefully studied the most powerful Arabian movement, that of the Wahhabi sect of fundamentalist Islam, then headed by Abdel-Aziz ibn Saud, the eventual founder of Saudi Arabia in the 1920s. For over thirty years, Philby was the liaison between London and King Saud. At first, Philby sought to harmonize the objectives of the Saudi family in eastern Arabia with the already established Hijaz movement of the Hashemite clan of the Sharif of Mecca, Hussein, who was then a paid agent of the Arab Bureau. Increasingly, however, Philby argued in British councils that London ought to throw its support behind ibn Saud, and eventually Saudi military victories in central Arabia won his argument for him.

The military strength of the Saudi family was based on a puritanical desert fundamentalist movement called the Ikhwan. Comprised of tribal leaders organized into clan militia and zealous in their Islamic faith, Ikhwan troops became the scourge of Arabia—with British arms. In later years, King Saud of Saudi Arabia came into conflict with the Ikhwan, and forced them to disband in the 1930s. Yet many believe that the Ikhwan, after its dissolution, continued to exist as a secret asset of British intelligence in Saudi Arabia, retaining its structure to this day. It is also believed that the current Saudi National Guard, the elite force commanded by the Muslim Brotherhood's Prince Abdullah ibn Abdel-Aziz, is comprised primarily out of the core group that formed the Ikhwan back in the 1930s.

In March 1919, Philby was appointed to the important Interdepartmental Eastern Committee established by Lord Curzon, and in early 1921, Philby and Lawrence lobbied with success for the formation of a separate Middle East Department in the Colonial Office. Involved then in the transactions of the British-Zionist

collaboration and the various ups and downs of London's
battle against the French and the U.S.S.R. in the Middle
East, Philby scuttled back and forth across Arabia living
a dissolute life, adopting Muslim customs (including
taking several wives), and eventually feigning conversion
to Islam. In this period, from the close of World War I to
the onset of World War II, not a single event of any
importance happened in Saudi Arabia without Philby's
knowledge and often approval. For instance, the securing by Standard Oil of California of the contract to
explore for oil in Saudi Arabia, which eventually established the Arabian-American Oil Company (Aramco),
was accomplished by the personal influence of Philby in
the Saudi Court.

Politically, Philby established for himself something
of a reputation of an oddball. During World War II, he
was openly pro-Hitler, often calling for the British to
halt the war against Germany, and joining the fascist
Peoples Party in England under Lord Tavistock. At the
same time, however, Philby carefully cultivated the guise
of an "anti-imperialist," arguing against the continuation of the empire after the war and supporting nationalist causes, especially Arab nationalism. It was at this
time, during and after World War II, that Philby began
to cultivate covert relations with the Soviet Union.
Stalin, of course, had no illusions about who Philby was
or what he represented, but to the extent that Philby
appeared to seek to dismantle the British Empire, Stalin
saw this as grounds for collaboration.

But Philby's contacts into the U.S.S.R. operated
through other, older and more subtle channels. As a
leading member of the Orientalists' Congress, Philby
came into close contact with leading Soviet scholars on

Islam, the Orient, the Arab world, and India. The Orientalists' Congress, held every few years in a different world capital, was a movement established in the 1880s and continued through the twentieth century as a joint project of British SIS and the Jesuits.

Later, before and after World War II, one of Philby's mentors and sponsors was Monseigneur Gonzague Ryckmans, a Jesuit priest from the Louvain University in Belgium. Ryckmans was one of the guiding lights of the Orientalists' movement and the editor of *Le Museon* of Louvain. Together with Ryckmans' son Jacques, the Philby-Ryckmans combination was almost perfectly symbolic of the Anglo-Jesuit strategic marriage in the Middle East, and the trio often toured Saudi Arabia together.

Part of what Philby and the Ryckmans family sought during this time was evidence of the existence of certain pre-Islamic Arabian movements. Exploring archeological sites and compiling massive notes, Philby and Ryckmans were looking for concrete "artifacts" on which to base the creation of a new, anti-Islamic movement linked to the ancient cult goddesses—like the cult of Allat which prevailed in Arabia before the coming of the Prophet Mohammed. It was cults such as these that fed into the mystical movements, and other anti-Islamic cults under Philby's supervision.

The Orientalists' Congress had come into existence precisely as Afghani's pan-Islamic movement was getting off the ground, and the movement called the "Indissoluble Bond of Afghani and Abduh" was spawning British freemasonic secret societies all over the Islamic world. Around the turn of the century, Afghani himself often visited Czarist Russia, where he came into contact with the forces in Russia that eventually became the leadership of the Trotskyite and Bukharinite wings of the Soviet Communist movement, the anarchists, the pan-Slav movement, and—especially—Russian scholars and specialists in Islam. Far from being exterminated during the Russian Revolution, Afghani's Russian networks survived to become Philby's collaborators.

Now, what of St.-John Philby's son?

Harold Adrian Russell Philby, born in India during his father's SIS service there, was nicknamed "Kim" after the boy in Rudyard Kipling's novel who goes to work for British intelligence to learn the "Great Game" of battling Russia for control of the Eurasian land mass. In the 1930s, Philby followed his father's footsteps and enrolled in Cambridge University's Trinity College. There, Kim Philby joined some friends in the secret society known as the Apostles Club. Among his colleagues were Donald Maclean, Guy Burgess, and Anthony Blunt—the latter a descendent of the famous Wilfrid S. Blunt of the nineteenth century Blunt-Browne team.

With his father's approval, Kim Philby was tracked into the communist and socialist movement during his college days, and he openly espoused the most radical social-reform and liberal causes of the pro-Soviet movement during this period. During a stay in Vienna, Austria, Kim Philby was *allegedly* recruited into a Soviet intelligence network in the early 1930s. Nevertheless, after a brief tour in Spain as a foreign correspondent—a job secured for him by his father—he was admitted into the British foreign intelligence service MI-6. At various points during his career, Kim Philby ran the Iberian Desk of MI-6, its Soviet Desk and, in the formative period of the CIA after World War II, was station chief for British intelligence in Washington, D.C.

In 1951, Philby was rumored to be involved in the defection of two of his friends and colleagues in MI-6, Burgess and Maclean, to the U.S.S.R. Despite these rumors, Philby was allowed to remain in active service in MI-6, during which period he was alleged to have been transmitting British and American secrets to Moscow. (In fact, while Philby undoubtedly delivered CIA secret information to the U.S.S.R., it is unlikely that he betrayed his British command by leaking anything of value to them!)

In 1955, however, Philby was publicly named as the "Third Man" in the spy scandal of Burgess and Maclean, and demoted from his post in MI-6 in London to the position of intelligence "stringer" in Beirut. In this position, Kim Philby continued to serve as a liaison between MI-6, the KGB, and various Arab and Israeli secret services. Ostensibly, after 1955 Philby was the Middle East correspondent of the London *Observer* and *The Economist*.

As soon as he arrived in Beirut, "Kim" Philby was introduced by St.-John Philby to the entire range of the father's Middle East contacts, from Saudi sheikhs and Jordanian Arab Legion commanders to Israeli Mossad agents and Lebanese spooks of all sorts.

Together, Philby and Philby traveled the Middle East. From 1955 until September 1960, St.-John Philby showed his son the ropes, in particular introducing Kim to the British Muslim Brotherhood networks in the Arab world, and to the extensive intelligence areas in which the British and Soviet intelligence services cooperated in supporting "leftist" and communist movements. The younger Philby soon became an intimate of various Arab Communist parties, the Iranian Tudeh Party, Lebanese leftist and Nasserite movements, and the Arab Baath Socialist Party faction of Michel Aflaq. In each of these movements, British SIS had a long history of infiltration and even effective overall control.

In September 1960 Harry St.-John Bridger Philby died. His last words were, "I am bored."

"Kim" Philby continued to work as British intelligence liaison in Beirut, constantly passing information (and, often, disinformation) to the KGB. In 1962-1963, the Middle East entered a serious crisis. In Iran, the British had launched their destabilization of the Shah, triggering riots and anti-Shah outbursts by backers of the Ayatollah Khomeini. Then, in January 1963, Kim Philby disappeared while on his way to a diplomatic party in Beirut. In the following month, February 8, the Baath party seized power in Syria; then, on March 8, the Iraqi government was overthrown by the same Baath party organization. Syria and Iraq began immediate talk about political unity, and the Anglo-American press predicted the imminent collapse of the pro-Western regimes in Jordan and Saudi Arabia. In the midst of this crisis, which reached panic proportions in certain Western capitals—particularly France, Italy, West Germany, and Japan—"Kim" Philby suddenly turned up, in April 1963, in Moscow. The master British spy and triple-agent, amid a Middle East crisis partly of his own making, had managed to "launder" himself into the U.S.S.R. itself.

From that point on, Philby has served as an active officer of the Soviet KGB. In 1978, when the Khomeini revolution was already underway in Iran, *The Journal*, publication of the Muslim Brotherhood-linked World Muslim League in Saudi Arabia, reported Philby's Soviet Foreign Ministry position as coordinator of policy toward Syria, Iraq, Jordan, and the Arabian Peninsula. In the following year, Philby was promoted, becoming General Philby of the KGB—the rank he holds today. During this period, the old Cambridge Apostle and Dark Ages activist exercised an untoward influence on Soviet policy toward the Khomeini revolution and the Arab world's Muslim Brotherhood.

The matter of Kim Philby, the "Third Man," has not yet been concluded as far as the intelligence establishment of the U.S.A. is concerned. The file remains open in more than one sense.

His defection in 1963 still raises questions which today are reflected in the ongoing search for the mythical "KGB mole" in high places in Washington. Other questions, raised about the "failure" of American intelligence to prevent Khomeini's rise to power, intersect the matter relating to the "KGB mole." What is the truth?

In general outline, the solution to this problem will eventually demonstrate the following: there is not, and there never was, a "KGB mole" problem as such. Instead, there is a certain grouping within the American intelligence community which from its inception during World War II, has been controlled by the British-Canadian-dominated Special Operations Executive of wartime fame. This grouping is clustered around certain powerful families and financial fortunes on the East Coast whose intelligence operating arm was shaped by the networks once created by Sir William Stephenson. These include the old Socialist Party, Jewish Labor Committee networks; the intelligence networks around Philby-trained James Jesus Angleton, Jay Lovestone, Irving Brown, Irving Suall of the Anti-Defamation League; the Fitzroy Maclean networks around the United Nations; the Canadian Jesuits' networks which run "liberation theology" operations in Latin America; the reascendent Jabotinsky-Revisionist wing in the Zionist movement; and the Muslim Brotherhood in Islam.

The British controllers of this U.S.-based network also control, in the Soviet Union, various parts of the Soviet intelligence establishment, including Georgi Arbatov's U.S.A.-Canada Institute—where Burgess and Maclean were employed—as well as those parts of the KGB and the Foreign Ministry where Philby is employed. These are the sectors of the Soviet administration obsessed with "Third World" liberation movement and class-struggle projects.

What seems to be an "intelligence leak" problem attributable to some mysterious "KGB mole," will in fact prove to be an arrangement whereby the preponderant section of U.S. intelligence, and a section of Soviet intelligence, are both controlled by the same overriding entity, the SOE-"Canadian" grouping within British intelligence. This would explain, among other things, how a fire-eating anticommunist like Mr. Brzezinski, a Canadian-Jesuit-trained operative, collaborated with the KGB to install Khomeini in power. The information is all buried in the yet-to-be-closed file of Harold Adrian Russell "Kim" Philby, the "Third Man."

Index

If You Want The History Behind

The Khomeini Conspiracy

You Will Want to Order These
Franklin House Titles:

The New Dark Ages Conspiracy

Carol White's explosive narrative of Bertrand Russell, H.G. Wells,
and Britain's plot to destroy civilization.   **$4.95.** Paper. Illus.

Will the Soviets Rule in the 1980s?

Lyndon LaRouche's indictment of the Council on Foreign Relations/
Trilateral Commission war-strategy for the 1980s.   **$3.95** Paper. Illus.

The Ugly Truth About Milton Friedman

Lyndon LaRouche and David Goldman dissect today's most dismal
economic fraud and who made him prominent despite a record
of disasters.   **$3.95** Paper. Illus.

What Every Conservative Should Know
About Communism

LaRouche offers Americans a new approach to the Soviet Union
by exposing the real history of the British creation of communism—
beginning with America's first communist, Thomas Jefferson.
                                                $3.95. Paper. Illus.

(All titles available from The New Benjamin Franklin House)

_____ copies of **The New Dark Ages Conspiracy**

_____ copies of **Will the Soviets Rule?**

_____ copies of **Ugly Truth About Milton Friedman**

_____ copies of **What Every Conservative Should Know**

The New Benjamin Franklin House Publishing Co., Inc.
c/o Campaigner Publications, Inc., Dept. BEB
304 West 58th Street, 5th floor
New York, N.Y. 10019

(All checks or money orders payable to The New Benjamin Franklin House)

Interested in other Franklin House titles? Write us for a catalogue.